GUID

C000109293

Edited by **Helen Paynter** and **David Spriggs**

The Bible Reading Fellowship
15 The Chambers, Vineyard
Abingdon OX14 3FE
brf.org.uk

The Bible Reading Fellowship (BRF) is a Registered Charity (233280)

ISBN 978 0 85746 997 7
All rights reserved

Distributed in Australia by:
MediaCom Education Inc, PO Box 610, Unley, SA 5061
Tel: 1 800 811 311 | admin@mediacom.org.au

Distributed in New Zealand by:
Scripture Union Wholesale, PO Box 760, Wellington
Tel: 04 385 0421 | suwholesale@clear.net.nz

Acknowledgements
Scripture quotations marked with the following acronyms are taken from the
version shown. Where no acronym is given, the quotation is taken from the version
stated in the contributor's introduction. ESV: The Holy Bible, English Standard
Version, published by HarperCollins Publishers, © 2001 Crossway Bibles, a division
of Good News Publishers. Used by permission. All rights reserved. NRSV: The New
Revised Standard Version of the Bible, Anglicised edition, copyright © 1989, 1995 by
the Division of Christian Education of the National Council of the Churches of Christ
in the United States of America. Used by permission. All rights reserved. TNIV: The
Holy Bible, Today's New International Version, copyright © 2004 by Biblica. Used by
permission of Hodder & Stoughton Publishers, a division of Hodder Headline Ltd.
All rights reserved. 'TNIV' is a registered trademark of International Bible Society.

Every effort has been made to trace and contact copyright owners for material used
in this resource. We apologise for any inadvertent omissions or errors, and would
ask those concerned to contact us so that full acknowledgement can be made in
the future.

A catalogue record for this book is available from the British Library

Printed by Gutenberg Press, Tarxien, Malta

Suggestions for using *Guidelines*

Set aside a regular time and place, if possible, when and where you can read and pray undisturbed. Before you begin, take time to be still and, if you find it helpful, use the BRF Prayer on page 6.

In *Guidelines*, the introductory section provides context for the passages or themes to be studied, while the units of comment can be used daily, weekly or whatever best fits your timetable. You will need a Bible (more than one if you want to compare different translations) as Bible passages are not included. Please don't be tempted to skip the Bible reading because you know the passage well. We will have utterly failed if we don't bring our readers into engagement with the word of God. At the end of each week is a 'Guidelines' section, offering further thoughts about or practical application of what you have been studying.

Occasionally, you may read something in *Guidelines* that you find particularly challenging, even uncomfortable. This is inevitable in a series of notes which draws on a wide spectrum of contributors and doesn't believe in ducking difficult issues. Indeed, we believe that *Guidelines* readers much prefer thought-provoking material to a bland diet that only confirms what they already think.

If you do disagree with a contributor, you may find it helpful to go through these three steps. First, think about why you feel uncomfortable. Perhaps this is an idea that is new to you, or you are not happy about the way something has been expressed. Or there may be something more substantial – you may feel that the writer is guilty of sweeping generalisation, factual error, or theological or ethical misjudgement. Second, pray that God would use this disagreement to teach you more about his word and about yourself. Third, have a deeper read about the issue. There are further reading suggestions at the end of each writer's block of notes. And then, do feel free to write to the contributor or the editor of *Guidelines*. We welcome communication, by email, phone or letter, as it enables us to discover what has been useful, challenging or infuriating for our readers. We don't always promise to change things, but we will always listen and think about your ideas, complaints or suggestions. Thank you!

To send feedback, please email **enquiries@brf.org.uk**, phone **+44 (0)1865 319700** or write to the address shown opposite.

Writers in this issue

Helen Paynter is a Baptist minister and tutor in biblical studies at Bristol Baptist College, where she also serves as director of the Centre for the Study of Bible and Violence. She is the commissioning editor of *Guidelines*.

Hazel Sherman is a Baptist minister, currently serving as one of the ministers of West Worthing Baptist Church. With a background in pastoral ministry and theological education, she has maintained a strong interest in academic theology and biblical studies and relishes opportunities for teaching and learning within a local congregation.

David G. Firth is a Baptist minister who is currently tutor in Old Testament at Trinity College Bristol. He is married and has three adult children.

Steve Motyer taught New Testament at London School of Theology and led the theology and counselling programme there before retiring in 2016. He is the author of a few books on the Bible and related themes, most notably on the second coming of Jesus. He is a proud father and grandfather and helps to lead his church in Watford.

Sally Nash is director of the Institute of Children, Youth and Mission and associate minister at Hodge Hill Church in Birmingham. She and her husband Paul blog at **markerpostsandshelters.wordpress.com**, often on things related to her week of notes.

Lucy Peppiatt is the principal of Westminster Theological Centre, where she also teaches Christian doctrine, spiritual formation and leadership. She writes on Christology, the Trinity, discipleship and women in the Bible.

Alec Gilmore, a Baptist minister and former director of Feed the Minds, has contributed to many Christian publications in the UK and US and has written extensively on Baptist and ecumenical affairs as well as biblical studies, including *A Concise Dictionary of Bible Origins and Interpretation* (T & T Clark/Continuum, 2006).

Ian Paul studied maths and worked in business before training for ordained ministry and completing a PhD on the interpretation of the book of Revelation. Following ten years in parish ministry and ten years in theological education, he now writes and teaches in a range of different contexts. He writes the well-known blog **psephizo.com**, is married to Maggie, and they have three adult children and a very cute dog called Barney.

Helen Paynter writes...

For many of us, the 'wild and wacky' parts of scripture – especially some of the more ecstatic parts of the prophetic writings – are something of a mystery. So I'm delighted in this edition of *Guidelines* to be able to introduce to you a new writer who will expertly guide us through one of those greatest mysteries – the book of Zechariah.

Hazel Sherman did her doctoral work on the book of Zechariah. In her notes she takes us through the book, helping us to understand some of the details of the prophet's words without losing sight of the big picture. As should be the case when we read the words of these passionate men of God, we will be deeply challenged by the message that the prophet brings us.

We are indeed fortunate to have real experts writing for us. I'm delighted that Steve Motyer has resumed his journey through Mark's gospel with us. I have found his notes very challenging and hope that you will, too. David G. Firth takes us through 2 Samuel, showing us how God is at work in the mess and muddle of realpolitik, Bronze-Age style. I also commend to you Ian Paul's helpful fortnight on 1 Timothy, and Alec Gilmore's study on Job and his friends.

We also have readings for Lent and Easter, of course. Sally Nash reflects on 21st-century approaches to discipleship and spirituality, and Lucy Peppiatt then picks up the baton and takes us through Holy Week and Easter week in a very lovely set of reflections that take us deeply into the contemplation of the person and work of Jesus Christ.

In response to the pandemic that hit us hard around the time that this edition was being prepared for press, I made the decision with BRF that we would switch out two weeks of notes for some reflections on the crisis and how we might respond to it. This is one of the greatest challenges that we are facing, as a world and as the church, in living memory, and it is important to reflect carefully on what God is saying to us in this time. There is a limit to what we can say in two weeks of reflections, but I hope that they will stimulate some prayerful contemplation.

So as another new year begins and we journey from the cradle to the cross, I pray that you will be blessed, challenged and inspired by these notes and the scriptures that they invite you into.

The BRF Prayer

Almighty God,
you have taught us that your word is a lamp for our feet
and a light for our path. Help us, and all who prayerfully
read your word, to deepen our fellowship with you
and with each other through your love.
And in so doing may we come to know you more fully,
love you more truly, and follow more faithfully
in the steps of your Son Jesus Christ, who lives and reigns
with you and the Holy Spirit, one God forevermore.
Amen

Were you there? BRF celebrates its centenary in 2022 and we'd love you to share your BRF memories with us. We've already heard from supporters with wonderful stories. Beryl Fudge attended our 25th anniversary service in Westminster Central Hall in 1947, in the presence of the Queen Mother and Princess Margaret. Catharine Heron was prepared for confirmation in 1945 by our founder, Canon Leslie Mannering, and still has his duplicated notes in their original brown cardboard folder.

Do you have a BRF story to tell, whether of events, people, books or Bible reading notes? Please email **eley.mcainsh@brf.org.uk**, call **01865 319708** or write to **Eley McAinsh** at BRF, 15 The Chambers, Vineyard, Abingdon OX14 3FE, United Kingdom.

Letters from lockdown

Helen Paynter

It's a standard primary school exercise: write a letter to your future self. Children are encouraged to imagine themselves when they are 'grown up', and offer some advice to that future person who is somehow them, yet somehow other. Of course, the results of such exercises can be quite amusing. Children tell their future selves that they hope they are famous footballers by now, or that they still love fairies.

In these notes I am attempting something similar, which could backfire badly. In May 2020 (now) I agreed with The Bible Reading Fellowship (BRF) that I would write two weeks of reflections on the Covid-19 crisis for *Guidelines*. The issue you are holding in your hand will have been sent to the printer at the beginning of June 2020. This makes it a risky endeavour. Who knows how much the world will have changed by the time you read this? But we have a sneaking suspicion that the issues will still be relevant.

So here are twelve reflections written at what I hope is the peak of the pandemic. To a certain extent, this is theology on the fly. We are being asked new questions that we haven't considered before. Objective appraisal of the situation that we are living through (and therefore mature theological reflection upon it) will not be fully possible for months or years.

But God's word does not change. So here are my reflections on the situation, as best I can offer them today. Maybe tomorrow I will be wiser, but the printer beckons. I offer them with some tentativity to my future self – to my future readers. I hope that they will provide some means of reflecting on what has been and what still is; on what might be and what could have been. Maybe the crisis will have passed, and we will have all returned to 'normal' – whatever that ever meant. If so, all well and good – but I'm willing to bet that God's word will still be relevant in 2021. I've staked more than this issue of *Guidelines* on it.

Unless otherwise stated, Bible quotations are taken from the ESV.

1 Disorientation

On the afternoon of 16 March 2020, my ministerial colleague and I had a lengthy phone call, discussing how we should best serve the church in the light of the developing coronavirus crisis. By 4.15 pm, we had a plan, and I felt an element of relief. At 5.00 pm I got into my car and drove home. On the way, I heard the live briefing from Downing Street, and the Prime Minister announcing that by the coming weekend, all those over 70 (which includes many of my congregation) and those with pre-existing health conditions (which included my husband and me) should go into strict self-isolation for 12 weeks. Within 45 minutes of our phone call, our plans had become redundant. I felt genuinely disorientated.

Walter Brueggemann describes certain of the psalms as being psalms of disorientation. These are psalms we use when all is not right with our world; when the world is not as it should be; when we experience grief or pain or bewilderment. There is something raw and beautiful and fundamentally honest about such psalms. Today's is one such example.

The sense of disorientation seems to pervade this psalm. 'Incline your ear, O Lord, and answer me,' cries the psalmist (v. 1), then declares, 'You, O Lord, are good and forgiving' (v. 5). But soon the rawness has crept in again – 'Show me a sign of your favour' – but then once again becomes 'You, Lord, have helped me and comforted me' (both in v. 17). This giddying cycle of emotions perhaps replicates our own sense of disorientation that we experience from time to time. It beautifully captures our whirling thoughts and the feelings that can flip so uncontrollably at times of shock and crisis.

In his analysis of psalms in this way, Brueggemann has helped us to understand that lament, plea and even challenge are all valid ways of approaching God. It is all prayer. It is all heard.

2 Known unto God

In Ezra and Nehemiah we have several lists of names. In Ezra 2 we find a numbered list of the first wave of returnees from exile. Chapter 8 has the names of the heads of houses who came with Ezra in a later wave. These are lists of those whose courage and faith would not allow them to remain comfortably in Babylonia, when there was work to be done rebuilding the walls of Jerusalem and re-establishing the temple there. The journey was long and arduous, and life when they arrived was like the Wild West – precarious, unsettled and uncomfortable. Here in Nehemiah 3, we have a different sort of list: a list of builders. These are the returnees who braved threat and physical hardship to cooperate in the reconstruction of the walls of Jerusalem. Each family's contribution is recorded and honoured. Boring as these lists of names might seem to be, I love the fact that they are recorded here. A roll of honour, a textual memorial – albeit an incomplete one. (Where are the women?)

We are all growing accustomed to seeing large numbers with reference to unnamed people. How many have died of Covid-19? How many have been infected? At the time of writing, we have just topped an estimated 60,000 in the UK who have lost their lives so far. It's an unimaginable number. How do we grieve 60,000 dead? How will our grief change when there are 80,000? And yet, if it doesn't, what does that say about the 'extra' 20,000? And so on.

But there are other lists, too. Or lists that don't exist, but should. The front-line workers who have willingly jeopardised their own safety in order to do essential work: to collect our rubbish, police our streets, care for our sick and elderly. Some of these have paid the ultimate price for their courage; they have all risked doing so.

It is unlikely that anyone will compile these lists in the years to come. But each name matters. Each life lost is grieved and grievable. Each life risked in the service of others is honourable. These textual memorials in Ezra and Nehemiah remind me that each name is known to the God who sees even the sparrows that fall from the sky (Matthew 10:29).

3 Terrors in the night

Our middle daughter used to experience night terrors when she was a small child. Every night, about half an hour after falling asleep, she would start screaming inconsolably. She wasn't awake – though she looked it. And that meant that I couldn't 'reach' her. I could put my arms around her, but she would either struggle out of them or just not respond to my attempts at comfort. She would look 'through' us, as if at something terrifying behind us. We just had to hold her and wait for the episode to pass.

It was at this time that I 'discovered' this psalm, though I must have read it dozens of times before. I was very struck by the recurring theme of dogs – probably a pack of jackals – returning and snarling by night (vv. 6, 14). It seemed an apt metaphor for what our daughter was experiencing, and the psalm became for me an immensely helpful prayer, until the terrors passed into history. My practice is to depersonalise the 'enemy' language of the psalms, and so I could pray against 'bloodthirsty men' (v.2) as a metaphor for the assaults we were currently experiencing.

For many of us, these last months have been a time of intense anxiety and strain. For many who struggle with pre-existent mental health issues, the problem has been even more intense. The metaphor of anxiety being like a dog that returns by night seems quite fitting. Other things come at night, too, especially if we are alone: regrets, recriminations and temptations – or physical symptoms such as breathlessness, pain and restlessness.

In the face of these 'dogs', God laughs (v. 8). Not *at* our suffering, of course. Never, for one minute. But at those things that seek to harm or disequilibrate his people – God laughs in the face of them (compare Psalm 2:4). They do not rattle him or perplex him; all things are in his hand. So with the psalmist, may we learn to say by night, 'O my Strength, I will watch for you' (v. 9), and when dawn finally breaks, 'I will sing aloud of your steadfast love in the morning' (v. 16).

4 'Gang aft agley'

Today's title is taken from one of the most famous lines of the Scottish poet Robbie Burns. In a fuller form, it is often (mis)quoted as, 'The best-laid plans of mice and men go oft awry.'

And yet, in functional terms, many of us have forgotten this. We have begun to imagine that we can order our own existence. We insulate ourselves from the climate in which we live, through air-conditioning and central heating – even in our cars. We are not at the mercies of the agricultural cycle because we stockpile food in our cupboards and our freezers. We protect our health through screening and good medical treatments. And as a result, we may have come to believe that we are impermeable. We expect that life will turn out well. And when it doesn't, we protest shrilly and cast about for who we can blame (hence, perhaps, the rise in medical negligence suits).

Of course, for many, both worldwide and in the UK – the poor, the chronically ill, those who live with political instability – this is far outside their experience or expectation. For them, these words of James ring true: 'You do not know what tomorrow will bring. What is your life? For you are a mist that appears for a little time and then vanishes' (4:14). But for perhaps the majority of Christians living in the west and global north in the last few decades, this verse has been more theoretical than matching our lived experience. And then, Covid-19 happened. Suddenly, our plans were disrupted. Holidays were cancelled. Working conditions altered. We incurred monetary loss or faced financial uncertainty. We experienced sickness, or knew we might. We faced the possibility of our own premature death. We lost those we love. We are not masters of our own fate. Our plans gang aft agley.

Though none of us would have chosen this crisis, it does present us with an opportunity to re-evaluate the way we live and the way that we think. As we emerge from it, we need to keep hold of the things we have learned in these days. The philosopher Judith Butler urges us to appreciate the precariousness of life, that condition of vulnerability that should lead us into interdependency in community. The apostle James got there first, though. As we struggle to re-equilibrate our lives, he warns us to do so with attention to those whose lives are even more precarious than our own (5:1–6).

5 The virus

One of the unanticipated blessings of lockdown has been the environmental benefits: the quality of the air, the clarity of the sky, the return of birdsong to our inner cities. We have even seen unexpected incursions of wild animals into usually busy public spaces. For a planet on the brink of climate crisis, this has offered a glimpse of hope. Could we return to a different 'normal'? Might our consumerist dependence on international travel and air-freight (for example) be exposed for the idolatry that it is?

These are complex issues with social, geopolitical, economic and scientific implications. The consequences for the planet might not be as wholly positive as the idealists among us would imagine. The economic cost of the pandemic might lead governments to pull back on commitments to climate change measures. The critical mass that the climate change rallies were gaining might dissipate.

In the light of the current crisis, various themes concerning the environment are emerging in popular discourse. One is that, finally, mother earth is 'taking back control'. In this narrative, humans are the virus, the blight on the earth. It is only a short stretch from here to the assertion that the 'cull' effected by the virus is a good thing; a disturbing idea, with the global death toll already in the hundreds of thousands.

On the other hand there are those who view the push-back of nature as a threat. Our hard-won dominance is losing ground. Such voices suggest that only the privileged romaticise nature because they are sheltered from its more dangerous excesses. Rather, nature is something to be controlled, harnessed and managed. Those who live with a more 'raw' experience of the climate and predators understand better than we do how much of a threat nature can be.

The biblical view of the relationship between humanity and nature begins in Genesis 1—3. Humanity *is* set above the rest of creation. We are not 'the virus'; we are its governors. But with the fall, the relationship is damaged. And, just as the male-female relationship becomes characterised by a mutual struggle for power (3:16), so too the relationship between humanity and creation has become one of mutual threat. Maybe a lesson that could emerge from these times is how to live more in the pattern of good governance that Genesis 1 sets out.

6 Hitting the wall

Acts 13:1–13

John Mark was a young, wealthy Jerusalemite (his mother owned a house large enough to accommodate prayer meetings; see Acts 12:12), who set out with Paul and Barnabas on Paul's first missionary journey (12:25). Although initially quite helpful to Paul (13:5), at Perga he abandoned them and returned home. Paul clearly viewed this as evidence of unreliability, since he resisted John Mark's involvement with a later missionary project (15:37–40).

So what exactly was the reason for John Mark's sudden departure? We know that the next leg of the journey would have taken them across the Taurus mountains, a rugged and bandit-ridden journey, which may lie behind Paul's words in 2 Corinthians 11:26. It has been suggested that malaria, or the fear of it, drove John Mark back. Whatever the exact circumstances, it is reasonable to conclude that he may have hit what is known, in terms of culture shock, as 'the wall'. Hitting the wall comes when the glamour has worn off the travel experience, language learning is proving hard and the sheer 'otherness' of the unfamiliar culture threatens to overwhelm. In mission work, it can lead to discouragement, doubt and sometimes the abandonment of the mission. Unexpected emotions arise, and normally concealed personality traits can emerge. There are a number of walls in the normal process of enculturation.

One of the most common expressions that I'm hearing at present is 'these strange times', closely followed by 'unprecedented'. Many of us feel as if we are in a different country. The rules and customs are different, our patterns of living have changed and even familiar places have suddenly been repurposed and now feel alien. And it is gradually dawning on us that this is not a twelve-week wonder. In one form or another, we are probably in this for the long-haul. For many of us, lockdown has been a long process of hitting a series of walls that could be compared with culture shock.

Advice to missionaries in such times is to push through the discomfort and to receive good pastoral care. Maybe John Mark failed to push hard enough. Maybe Paul was struggling with his own wall and failed to support his protégé. But the story has a happy ending, as Paul later commends him to the church in Colossae (Colossians 4:10), describes John Mark as a co-worker (Philemon 24) and considers him 'very useful' (2 Timothy 4:11). Thanks be to the God of forgiveness, who brought reconciliation and restitution and used both men, despite their struggles with the wall.

Guidelines

Scholars speculate about which city Paul was detained in when he wrote the letter to the church in Philippi. While we aren't sure what his circumstances were like, Peter's imprisonment in Jerusalem (Acts 12) describes him being in chains. In Rome, Paul was probably under something more like house arrest. But whatever his exact situation, it is striking how Paul refuses to allow his vision to be constrained by the four walls within which he is confined. His mind reaches beyond the four walls in which he is trapped, both physically as he prays for his friends (Philippians 1:9–10), and metaphorically as he fixes his mind on eschatological hope (v. 11).

It is tempting during times of crisis to allow our worldview to shrink to our own personal issues and those of our nearest and dearest. But we have nothing like Paul's excuse for such myopia. Flawed as technology is, it has opened up extraordinary opportunities for engagement with loved ones, colleagues and even total strangers. And while it is not within reach of everyone in our society, I'd guess that most readers of *Guidelines* have internet capability.

Be that as it may, we would do well to heed Paul's example as he reaches out in love and prayer towards his absent friends in Philippi. As he says in his letter to the church in Corinth, 'Besides everything else, I face daily the pressure of my concern for all the churches. Who is weak, and I do not feel weak? Who is led into sin, and I do not inwardly burn?' (2 Corinthians 11:28–29, NIV). One lesson I am hoping to learn in this time is to have a broader vision, despite my current physical restrictions of movement.

1 No one is an island

1 Corinthians 12:12–26

We must be cautious about misapplying scripture for our own purposes, and Paul is certainly not writing about wider society here. But if the church is to be understood as an eschatological foretaste of the new heavens and earth, it should function as a sign and pointer to that reality. So perhaps Paul's words here can give us a clue about how our communities could be, at their best.

Our current circumstances are drawing our attention more acutely to the way that society operates. Our complete dependence on low-income (but often highly skilled) workers has become clearer in these times. Most of the 'essential workers' fall into this category. Their work is often unseen, unglamorous and poorly paid. But we have, collectively, been drawn into a dystopian thought experiment: what if we didn't have bin collectors, utility workers or those who maintain payrolls and social security payments?

And our interdependency has become clearer, too – not only in the network of paid workers, but also in our mutual need for support. Many of us have had to rely on friends, neighbours and even strangers bringing food and medicines to the door. And mutual care is wider than that. The 'social contract' within which we operate has become apparent. The vast majority of us have been willing to accept severe curtailment of our rights to gather and travel, not primarily for our own protection but for the protection of the weaker and more vulnerable people in our society.

And there has been something beautiful about the communal lament that we are sharing. We have grieved the loss of national celebrities, but also the unknown people. The faces of health workers who have died have been in the newspapers; there has been outrage and grief at deaths in care homes; just this week a national newspaper ran a large article about the death of a young woman with severe learning difficulties. Perhaps we have become a little more tender-hearted; if one part of the body is in pain, it all hurts.

Those of us who are citizens not only of this society, but also of that eschatological union that is the church, might reflect on what we have learned from our communities during this crisis. How can we grow in the honour we pay those who do menial work, our interdependency and our shared care for the weakest?

2 Opportunity knocks?

Philippians 1:12–26

There has been plenty of discussion in online forums, particularly those frequented by church leaders, of the 'opportunity for church growth' afforded by the pandemic. While the closure of church buildings has presented many challenges, the move to online services, which are only encircled by virtual boundaries that are easier to cross, has opened the church up to people who would never normally darken our doors. Further, we are seeing the well-known phenomenon that crisis tends to evoke a pondering about the deep spiritual realities of life, and a grappling towards the transcendent. All in all, the pandemic might well be described as an 'opportunity'.

But for many, there is something distasteful about this language. This moment is being named as an 'opportunity' in the midst of the grief of millions, who have not only lost loved ones, but – in many cases – have been unable to be present with them in their last hours. It is being named as 'opportunity' in the midst of intense global fear and anxiety. And it is being named as 'opportunity' in the setting of a financial crisis that will bring unemployment and ruin for many; and in the setting of a lockdown that is sharply exacerbating abusive situations and mental health struggles. Talking about 'opportunity' seems insensitive, to say the least.

Here, perhaps, the example of the apostle Paul can be helpful for us. Trapped in prison, probably within Rome, he could easily have succumbed to despair at the disruption of his vital work. Rather, his response is one of joy (1:18; 2:1–2; compare Colossians 1:24; 2 Corinthians 12:9–10; Romans 5:3–5). But we should note two things. First, he notices *what God is doing* because of his circumstances (vv. 12-14). This is not gleeful empire building, but rather a fresh realisation that God turns all things to good (compare Genesis 50:20; Romans 8:28). And second, this noticing and expectation of God's good purposes is being expressed in the context of his own intense experience of it. The chains are on *his* hands, and the head that will be on the block is *his* own.

In our anticipation of the good things that God will do, despite and through these circumstances that afflict us, we would do well to focus at least as much on identification with the lowest and least, as on opportunities for extending our own influence.

3 Zero-sum gain

1 Kings 17:8–16

In May 2020, the editor of the world-famous medical journal *The Lancet* published an article publicly berating himself for failing to commemorate the 40th anniversary of the global eradication of smallpox. He had been distracted, he noted, by the pressing concerns of the Covid-19 pandemic. While the commemoration of a historical event might seem an excusable lapse under the circumstances, he used the instance to explore the neglect of other current needs. 'Responding to Covid-19 must not be a zero-sum game… This coronavirus is exploiting and accentuating existing health crises worldwide' (Richard Horton, *The Lancet*, vol. 395, issue 10236, p. 1534, 16 May 2020).

His point has application well beyond the medical world. Understandably, huge resources (financial and human) have been diverted into the search for ways of controlling and mitigating this great threat. But other needs have not gone away. Indeed, as Horton indicates, they may be exacerbated by the pandemic. While we fret about the virus, global weather catastrophes are still happening. Wars are still being waged. Other diseases are still wreaking havoc. Governments may be taking advantage of our distraction to bring in unpopular, perhaps dangerous, legislation through the back door. Persecution of our Christian brothers and sisters (and of many other faith groups) is still ongoing. And so on.

It might be tempting to focus on what seems most pressing and defer other matters until later. But this, as Horton points out, would be to allow the virus to strike us twice. Rather, we need to allow our hearts to expand to accommodate these new needs without abandoning the old ones. If this is true for society as a whole, how much more should it be true for a people whose faith is in the God who allowed the oil and flour to continue as long as the crisis did (v. 16)? The widow's sacrificial support for the prophet resulted in a more than zero-sum gain. The small offering of a few loaves and fish became in the hands of Jesus a feast for thousands. Love is not divided with the birth of a new baby in the family, but multiplied. This is the economy of the kingdom of God.

4 Toilet roll hoarding

Verse 11 is almost certainly familiar to you. It is used as an inspirational quotation on a million bookmarks and a thousand memes around the internet: 'I know the plans I have for you, declares the Lord, plans for welfare and not for evil, to give you a future and a hope.' As we so often do in the western church, we have tended to read this as if it were all about us. *Our* prosperity. *Our* future.

But as always, it's important to read it in context. The background is the Babylonian exile. God's people have been scattered as a direct result of their disobedience, just as they had been warned about. It's about ancient Judah and their covenant disobedience (Deuteronomy 28:47-68). It's not all about us.

In fact, 'it's not all about you' could be described as the theme of Jeremiah's letter. How are the exiled people to live in the strange new world in which they find themselves? The temptation could be to look after number one – their own people, their own community. They'd been swept away by forces beyond their control. Why shouldn't they consider first their own security and comfort? They'd had precious little of either in the preceding few years. But Jeremiah's letter called them to attend to the welfare of the whole community – the place where they had found themselves marooned on the tide of history. And indeed, within that 'whole community' would have been those whom they identified as enemies – even, perhaps, the soldiers who led the assault and their families.

Taken in its particular place in salvation history, there is a particular purpose to Jeremiah's letter. The exiles were to settle down in Babylonia and let the requisite years pass until God's word of comfort (Isaiah 40:1–2) came. But there are things we too can learn from this long-dead prophet about how to respond when the tide of events threatens to overwhelm us, whether that is in the context of a global pandemic or a personal tragedy: seek the welfare of the place where you are right now.

The early church understood this. Building on their early days, when they enjoyed 'favour with all the people' (Acts 2:47), they soon became renowned for their care for the poor, their willingness to bury the dead (even in time of plague) and their adoption of unwanted infants who had been abandoned to the elements and wild animals.

In crisis, as in times of prosperity, it's not all about us. Hoarding toilet roll will not do. Rather, we are called to work for the welfare of all, even when that is personally costly. And even when the 'all' includes toilet-roll hoarders.

5 Stunted imaginations

Matthew 6:19–34

As always, the sermon on the mount packs a punch. Today I'd like to focus simply on those few words in verse 21: 'Where your treasure is, there your heart will be also.'

Judith Butler, a critical theorist whom I have already referred to, described the concept of 'grievability' – what are the deaths that a society considers worthy of grief? This might be considered a test of a society's values.

The World Health Organisation estimates that over 400,000 people died of malaria in 2018. Around 144 million children under five are stunted in their growth because of malnutrition. I could go on. Of course, these are not part of a rapidly escalating pandemic. And many of us support organisations that seek to mitigate these ills, while most western governments have overseas aid budgets (which are closely tied up with trade agreements). But if we are honest, the indignation, consuming anxiety and determination with which we are confronting the Covid-19 crisis vastly exceeds our response to these other health crises – because they mainly affect people who aren't like us and whose pain we somehow struggle to imagine.

'Where your treasure is, there your heart will be also.' I'm not sure those words are done with us yet. Here's something else I have noticed in these times – and I describe my own response as much as anyone else's. The inconveniences we lament – being unable to gather with friends, being unable to buy things we want or have maintenance work done on our properties, even some of our financial anxiety – are the everyday realities of life for many in our own country, and even more so in global terms. For many who are immuno-compromised, severely incapacitated or very elderly, getting out and about are luxuries or unattainable. Things that we regard as barely tolerable (like the damp patch spreading in the wall that adjoins my shower) are wildly beyond the reach of those who live in precarious accommodation, refugee camps or shanty towns. Even our ridiculous preoccupation with toilet roll reveals our incapacity to imagine what life is like for the billions of people who do not have toilets in their homes.

I find myself ashamed as I write these words, and I resolve to do better. Because where our heart is – the things that we become indignant or dismayed about – reveals where we have placed our treasure. Lord, grow our imagination for the woes of others.

6 Where is your faith?

You have probably seen coverage of protests, mainly in the USA, with Christians waving banners with slogans such 'Jesus is my vaccine', asserting the right to assemble and demanding the reopening of their churches. We could discuss such protests in relation to the language of entitlement and rights, and consider what loving our neighbours looks like during a pandemic. But let us, rather, begin with the claim that true faith will protect the believer from the virus.

It is abundantly clear in scripture that while faith sometimes brings healing (Mark 2:5; 5:34; James 5:15), it does not always (the book of Job; 2 Corinthians 12:7–9). To make such a claim without nuance is not only foolish and unscriptural, but it also negates the suffering and death of many faithful believers.

The letters to the seven churches in Revelation were addressed to believers in a time of great crisis – not pandemic, but sharp persecution. It is striking that nowhere in the book are they promised that faith will exempt them from the time of trial. Rather, they are promised that God will hold them *in* their trials and that he will one day make an end to all evil. The language of faith, where it is used, mainly refers to faithfulness, to the dogged refusal to go under when the waves of suffering come crashing down again and again, and the courageous refusal to collude with evil powers, even where that might mean a mitigation of suffering. Hence each church is encouraged with a promise offered 'to the one who conquers' (2:7, 11, 17, 26; 3:5, 12, 21).

We should be cautious when we claim 'faith', because it places us in a great bind before God. In verse 19, the seer couples faithfulness with other qualities: 'I know your works and your love and faithfulness and service and steadfastness' (my translation). We might also recall the words of Paul: 'If I have all faith, so as to remove mountains, but have not love, I am nothing' (1 Corinthians 13:2).

Rather than using the language of 'faith' to make a defiant claim upon promises we have not been given, true faithfulness means a steadfast determination to hold on to the promises we have and to serve God and others with patient love in the meantime.

Guidelines

How long do your New Year's resolutions last? Most of mine don't get beyond the end of January.

I said in the introduction to these two weeks of notes that this is a risky endeavour for me. It's impossible to guess at the time of writing what our circumstances will be like in January, when you read them. It may be that my reflections feel rather quaint – a word from a distant past, a semi-forgotten horror.

But if this is the case, I'd challenge you to recall what your own reflections were during that time. What were the things that you resolved to do better? What changes did you vow to make? Is it possible that promises you made to God in June, or August, or October, have already dissipated in a new, relaxed world?

If this might be the case, then perhaps this week's notes will help you reclaim those promises: to re-enter the precarity, anxiety and tenderness of the pandemic and retrieve what was good and what ought to be remembered. May God be sowing good seed in us all in these days, and may we have the wisdom and tenacity to nurture it in our lives.

An unfamiliar familiarity: keeping company with Zechariah

Hazel Sherman

Zechariah may be a little-known book to Christian readers, though it contains some specific quotations and allusions which are well-known from references in the New Testament. To read it at one sitting is to be surprised by a sense of 'I've heard that before', but also to be baffled by the strangeness of its imagery, and the reader who wishes to discern a word for their own time and situation will be aware of many 'so what?' questions.

When we try to navigate the prophetic book on its own terms, we find ourselves in an unfamiliar landscape. In fact, it may be helpful to allow for more than one landscape – for even if the physical geography is the same, there is a shift in political and theological landscape between chapters 1—8 and chapters 9—14.

This much is clear: the eponymous author is a contemporary of Haggai (Ezra 5:1), working during the time of Ezra and Nehemiah around 520BC, likely among the priests (Nehemiah 12:16). The context of Zechariah 1—8 is that of the rebuilding and restoration of the temple and its high priesthood, which is portrayed as a magnet for the nations (Zechariah 8:23).

While the climax at the end of chapters 9—14 is also God's bringing universal hope in and from Jerusalem, a variety of views are held on dating and situation, from the mid-eighth century BC to as late as 250 years before the time of Christ. There are differences in style and content to what has gone before. The text itself gives no reference to its dating, and many scholars speak of a 'second Zechariah'. However, the quest for a specific setting is not altogether the same as the quest for meaning, and as we read we can be alert to themes which transcend any one historical context.

It is not easy to answer the question, 'What did this mean for the first hearers?', and sometimes harder to answer, 'What does it mean for me, today?' I hope some of the thoughts shared in these notes will encourage you to develop some responses to your own questions of the passages.

Unless otherwise stated, Bible quotations are taken from the NRSV.

1 The prophetic word and two visions

Zechariah 1

The people are called to return and learn from the consequences of their 'evil ways' (v. 4). God's anger against former generations is being worked out, and the present generation is being offered a chance to get things back on their right basis. The plea for return, either to escape or recover from retribution, is routine in the biblical witness, but a series of visions in Zechariah take us into stranger territory. Like bookends to these visions, the riders with their horses and chariots patrol the whole earth (1:7–11; 6:1–8). God is not just concerned with one people group, however fundamental they are in his providence, but with the affairs of the whole world.

There may be an irony in the report that 'the whole earth remains at peace' (v. 11), for how can it really be at peace when nations sit back and take their ease in the face of impending disaster (v. 15)

Who are the horsemen? The significance of their horses' colourings have been variously interpreted, for example, red for judgement, white reflecting joy and triumph, and sorrel as a mixed state of prosperity and approaching wrath. Among Christian commentators there has often been a leaning into allegory, with the man on the red horse representing Christ coming in judgement, or the sorrel representing the incarnation. They may remind us of the four living creatures of Ezekiel 1:5–12, and the horsemen of the apocalypse in Revelation 4 and 6 are redolent with Zechariah's imagery, though not identical with it. Revelation's horsemen are agents of judgement, whereas in Zechariah they are limited to patrolling the earth. But finding them there alerts us to the potential of a text to develop beyond its own time.

It is as true for the prophets of the Bible as it is for any preacher that a word once uttered no longer speaks only with its author's voice. Zechariah speaks beyond itself with or without the prophet's specific intent, and to recognise this may draw some humility from us if we are tempted to assume that there is only ever one 'right' reading.

At the end of the passage we are reading today, almost as if by sleight of hand, the prophetic imagination moves from horses to blacksmiths. The powerful nations symbolised by a horn (v. 19; compare 1 Kings 22:11; Psalm 75:10; Ezekiel 29:21) will be destroyed by workers who are equipped for their task.

2 Measurements of restoration and leadership

The prophet is questioning his interpreter. It is as if he sees things he does not understand and, unlike some of the earlier prophets, does not speak so directly as God's mouthpiece. Perhaps through the existential upheavals and uncertainties of exile and cross-cultural challenges a more veiled sort of communication is emerging, where God's direct speech is mediated through angelic messengers.

He asks the man with the measuring line what he is doing, but the reply he gets is corrected by a second angel. The first impression is that he is going to measure the dimensions of Jerusalem (2:2), but there is an almost immediate shift as the need for measurement seems to be done away with. Measurement speaks of containing, of delineating an area or a territory. It enables a sense of 'inside' and 'outside', an arena of safety and protection distinguished from a ground of threat and alienation. The man with the measuring line may think he is going to record dimensions, but that will be unnecessary, since when God's glory both indwells and surrounds Jerusalem the need for human boundaries will be done away with (2:4). Jerusalem with its temple and priesthood restored is a sign of things to come, when many nations will be drawn there together. In an interlude between the visions, the exiles are urged to make every effort to return to Jerusalem, which is affirmed again as the place from which God will rule.

Following the vision of a restored place comes a vision of restored and responsible leadership. The prophet is shown something like a court scene, with the high priest under investigation. The Hebrew 'Satan' is not a proper name here, but the description of a role which we might say conflates the work of the investigating officer with the xounsel for the prosecution. We have met him before, in Job 1:6–7, on the lookout for potential miscreants. The characterisation owes something to the coterie of courtiers surrounding the divinity in other literature of the ancient Near East, and it should not be confused with Jesus' antagonist and opponent of the church in the New Testament. Here, he is a figure drawing attention to the need for cleansing from a situation; there is no suggestion that Joshua himself has done wrong, but that, as one rescued from exile, he is representative of that whole tainted generation and made fit to lead the people into a renewed life.

3 Lampstands, olive trees and flying scrolls

Zechariah 4:1—5:4

The visions continue apace, and the prophet, newly awakened, requires a fresh calibration of his inner eye. The angel seems exasperated that Zechariah does not immediately grasp the significance of what he sees. Some have suggested that the lampstand is a menorah, as described within the tabernacle (Exodus 25:31–40), but If we avoid getting diverted by the seven branched candlesticks familiar from many modern windowsills, we might picture one stem holding a bowl with oil to feed the seven lamps round its perimeter, each with seven wicks. The light from this would be considerable and require a quantity of fuel, provided by the olive trees. But there is more, as the angelic interpreter explicates the seven lights as representing the range of God's sight (4:10b) and the two trees as those who stand by him to serve in kingly and priestly roles (4:14). God's presence is within the restored community but also transcends it in illumination and vision.

A direct address to Zerubbabel, who has returned with the exiles from Babylon as governor of Judea, comes between the vision and its explanation (4:6–7). Although it disrupts the flow of the text, set in-between it may serve to highlight the human agent through whom God is working.

As a child, one of my most used gifts was a Spirograph set. With care and patience it was possible to discover intricate detail within the simplest of shapes while apparently going round in circles. The mathematical principles which lay behind it escaped me, but that did not stop me from relishing the discovery of more depth in design at every turn. It may be helpful to think of this when seemingly going round in circles with Zechariah's text. For now, we move to a sixth vision: the flying scroll sent out as the instrument of God's curse to destroy the house of the thief and the perjurer. This vision may move us from temple to Torah. The furnishings and worship ritual of the temple, and the hearing and doing of the law which resides there in written form, are together at the heart of the restoration, and there will be dire consequences for those who ignore it.

4 A woman in a basket and four chariots

The circle turns again, and the removal of iniquity itself follows through from the removal of thieves and those who have borne false witness.

Some translations, reading *ephah* as a measurement of grain or to describe a container for grain, depict wickedness (represented as a woman) sitting in a basket with a lead cover. Such a basket would be too small to carry a human, so some translators prefer to use words like 'barrel', 'tub' or 'large container'. But strict realism is not really at the heart of reading passages like these, and the unrealistic confines may have the effect of making wickedness look cramped and ridiculous.

Grammatically, the word for wickedness (*rishah*) is a feminine noun, and it is not unreasonable to find it personified as female. But given centuries of misogynistic readings, and modern confusion of gender and grammar, it brings problems for the present reader who is ambivalent about the portrayal of the feminine as iniquitous, and suspects any reading which conforms uncritically to gender stereotypes.

We might notice, in passing, that there are two other women in this vision, who lift the basket and fly away with it. The word describing their wings as those of a 'stork' (*chasidah*) chimes with *chasid*, or as practising kindness and steadfast love (*chesed*). Without building a sermon from it, we might want to consider whether we will read this as a balance within the text, where women who are faithful to God are removing the evil that threatens God's people. However, storks are also named among the unclean creatures in Leviticus 11:19 and Deuteronomy 14:18, and it could be that the goddess-worship of the surrounding nations is under attack, as the unclean swoop down, bearing the basket away to be set on a base which sounds suspiciously like an idol's plinth.

Considerable activity in these visions is taking place 'in the air': not just the flying scroll and the basket of wickedness, but now the horses, which, like the four winds, are 'impatient to get off and patrol the earth' (6:7), complementing the earlier vision in 1:8–17. The earth is not the only sphere of divine engagement, and we are invited to continue to look beyond present boundaries.

5 Concluding action and messages

Among the returning exiles are those who are bringing with them gold and silver. Is this what they have managed to smuggle out? Is it a sign of their prosperity during exile, now transferred to the community who have struggled for years with few resources? Was it even theirs to bring? Each of these questions may rest behind the collection and use of the precious materials which will crown the signs of God's presence through the priesthood and monarchy. Despite the immediate connection of 'branch' with David's lineage, the high priest Joshua receives the crown: we have two figures in the scene and, though not confused, they are to some extent merged. There is uncertainty among translators here. 'Crown' is given in plural form, and some see scope in the text for both ruler and priest being crowned. Perhaps here is one of the signs of a growing discernment that, while ultimate authority belongs to God, God's wisdom calls for co-workers. If there is significance in the 'peaceful understanding' between priest and ruler, there is further vision-within-vision going on. A hint of this has already been glimpsed in 3:8. Exile, ultimately, is not separation from God, but becomes another route to discovering God's providence, and this providence calls in a whole range of participants.

Return of itself does not mean that all questions are answered. Just two years after the prophet has envisaged God's presence in the centre of a restored Jerusalem, and as the reconstructive work described in Ezra and Nehemiah begins to be evident, representatives from Bethel come to ask whether the ritual fast and mourning over the destruction of Jerusalem should continue, now that it is being rebuilt. They receive an answer by way of another question: what's the point of your fasting? The people are asked to consider their motivation. Reminded of God's unwavering commitment to truth, kindness, mercy and justice (7:9–10), the implication for the questioners seems to be 'it all depends on whether you will practise how I really want you to live'. When we move on to the next chapter, we will find a more direct statement of God's requirement to live with integrity, loving truth and peace (8:16–17).

6 Promise and culmination

Zechariah 8 paints a pastoral panorama of health and well-being. After the visionary detail of the preceding pictures, it is as if we have re-entered a landscape where we can admire the view without a furrowed brow.

As it was at the beginning of the book, 'Thus says the Lord of hosts; I am very jealous for Jerusalem and for Zion' (1:14), now it is proclaimed again: 'Thus says the Lord of hosts: I am jealous for Zion with great jealousy, and I am jealous for her with great wrath' (v. 2). Through everything there is this constant that, ultimately, God is not going to let his people go. More than that, his presence will draw all peoples, even in their strength (v. 22).

Part of the value of idealism in literature is to capture something of the universal yearning for a better world and use it as a palette for painting on the canvas of present reality. The public spaces of the city which once bore witness to death and distress (compare Jeremiah 49:26; 50:30) now become places filled with the aged at rest and the young at play (vv. 4–5). Such a picture speaks to the yearning of a people for whom the ideal is being eclipsed by the daily struggle.

If we are tempted to read this chapter as a stand-alone, as if the context was not one of daily work which seems to lead nowhere, squabbles and disagreements, disaffection and corruption, we might remember Ezra and Nehemiah and those who laboured with them. After the initial euphoria of the return (Ezra 1—3) came an uphill struggle to recover an identity of faith and practice, and the material struggle to rebuild the city walls is reflected in Nehemiah, including enthusiastic beginnings and setbacks (Nehemiah 3—4).

We might also remember that their search for the ideal was marred by a narrowness and ethnocentricity which itself needed to be challenged by subsequent people of faith. The book of Ruth may well originate as a protest against an ideal pushed beyond its compassionate limits, as the boundaries and imaginations of a restored people are stretched again in a foundation story of foreign blood in David's line.

Think about idealism, and how it features in your life and in the life of your church.

Guidelines

- Zechariah keeps company with the many Old Testament prophets when he speaks about God's anger towards his people. We live in an angry world, where we often misappropriate that sense of anger at wrongness and divert it into rage against anyone in our way or into self-destruction. Anger and wrath are words which we do not want to hear, but they represent the impulse for justice which is ineradicable in the Bible. How, from our Christian context, do we work against injustice whilst not feeding the world's anger?

- How do we deal with detail and yet grasp a larger and more nuanced picture? A fundamental problem of a reading that does not 'look beyond' its parameters is that it remains informative rather than becoming transformative. For example, the lampstand's dimensions and specific details in chapter 4 might either lead us into useless fact-checking or invite us into a meditative journey. Set some time aside to reflect on how, during this week, you have welcomed the all-seeing wisdom of God, and when you have preferred not to have your actions too clearly illuminated.

- It is not easy to live with the conviction that God brings restoration out of disaster. The excitement of returning home is soon followed by the reality of despondency in tasks to be done. The apostle Paul would later exhort his readers to remember that 'all things work together for good for those who love God' (Romans 8:28), but, like the exiles, we too need a multiplicity of signs. The sense of being 'special' is one of those things in life that can either equip us to live with more breadth and compassion or cause us to draw our horizons closer around ourselves. We do well to ask ourselves how this tension is played out in our own lives.

- And a question from the very last verse of this section: how might Zechariah 8:23 describe a missionary impulse for sharing the love and compassion of God in the present day?

1 The prophet's burden

Zechariah 9

At the beginning of this chapter we hear echoes of Amos', Isaiah's and Jeremiah's oracles against surrounding nations. Those who behaved as if they were invincible are getting their comeuppance. As we read on, we might be tempted to turn the pages quickly, having heard it before. Zechariah, though, while he may be echoing or repeating lists of prideful nations, is describing the complete disruption of all former, present or future power structures. We are reading something on the way to what has been called 'apocalyptic' literature, where eternal clues are deliberately set into temporal oppressive realities.

Expectations of who is in control are overturned. The destruction of Israel's historic enemies is the prelude to what God is doing, as into the desolation rides a triumphant and victorious king, 'humble and riding on a donkey, on a colt, the foal of a donkey' (v. 9). The gospel witness of Matthew and John will take this up when they describe Jesus entering Jerusalem. This is familiar to us, but we may not like its sequel in Zechariah. The Abraham and Mosaic covenants are evoked (v. 11) but then disrupted by the horror of the people themselves drinking the blood of their conquered oppressors (v. 15), before the picture rolls on to a pastoral idyll where all is well with the community whom God has saved (vv. 16–17). It is the responsibility of the reader to decide how the overturning of oppressive powers can be lived into as a story which keeps justice and peace as equal participants without slipping into vengeance. Unlike the prophet's first hearers, we have the further resource of Jesus at his last supper (Mark 14:24) holding justice and peace together through his living and dying.

How can the dual aspect of disaster and restoration not be a burden for the prophet? The first line of chapter 9 is often arranged by translators to become a heading: 'An oracle. The word of the Lord is against the land of Hadrach.' But the first word simply means 'burden' (as also at 12:1). Zechariah is with the prophets of every generation who cannot escape a sense of impending doom, even as they remain 'prisoners of hope'. Think of the speeches of Greta Thunberg to world leaders: her world view is that of a young woman in the 21st-century western world, but the passion and repetition which mark her addresses might help us come closer to the conviction of this prophet.

2 Promise of restoration and reverberating fear

Zechariah 10:1—11:3

As we have noticed before, there is much here that can be found elsewhere. The prophet repeats the familiar analogy of people being like sheep without a shepherd (as do Jeremiah and Ezekiel) and deplores the vacuity of those to whom they look for guidance. It raises the question of how we look for answers, or how we discern God's will in our personal and community lives. There is a huge contrast between the omnipotence of the creator who resources everyone and everything (10:1) and the sources which the population turns to in panic. They should know better than look to household gods, images representing ancestors, diviners and dreamers who represent a way of trying to future-proof one's interests without any corresponding moral or ethical anchor.

Times and empires move through Zechariah 10 like white-water rafting; the raft is lifted but comes crashing down again as the moment of safety passes and even their leaders ('shepherds') are not just weak but weakened further by God's deliberate action. Those who are struggling to survive are being thrown about even more. We could find an analogy in current TV science-fiction. In a recent episode of *Doctor Who*, the Doctor and her cohort are tricked by 'the Master' (a Time Lord who uses his power for destruction rather than salvation) into boarding a plane with an explosive device strapped to the seat in place of the pilot. As it hurtles down, we are paralysed with fear for not only the Doctor and her human helpers but also the whole human race. Who is in control?

Despite everything, God will 'visit' his flock (10:3). In other words, he will continue to pay attention to them. The Hebrew word *paqad* ('visit, attend to') is shaded differently in different circumstances. The NRSV chooses to translate the Hebrew with 'the Lord of hosts *cares for* his flock', but the sense of visitation is an activity which can be negative or positive. God is one who pays attention, practically, to what rulers and ruled alike are getting up to. Here in Zechariah, the same word is used to describe both the attention God will pay to his flock and what he will do to their leaders (NRSV: *punish*). We might think of the ironic distinction between any who will breathe a sigh of relief when attention is paid to their plight, while others will do all they can to avoid scrutiny.

3 Two shepherds

The harsh glare of the spotlight continues to fall on the consequences of a failed leadership. Rather than look for evidence of specific times and rulers, we might reflect on and absorb the sense of living in an impossible situation. A last chance has been offered, but it does not divert the inevitable: the rich build their wealth at the expense of the flock and praise God for the fruits of their corruption. It's a no-win situation, which won't even be helped by the intervention of a good shepherd, who will be rejected and replaced by a worthless shepherd.

Despite using his two 'sticks' for defence and guidance – one representing God's characteristic 'Favour' and other that 'Unity' which is God's will for his divided flock – the good shepherd is unable to make a difference, and God's favour (sometimes described as 'grace') no longer defines them and holds them together (v. 10). The shepherd is paid for his work, but he throws his derisory fee into the temple treasury, and as the coins clatter down he breaks his second staff 'Unity' (vv. 13–14). The gospel according to Matthew will shift the shape of the image as he portrays the activity of the betrayer, who asks for and receives his 30 pieces of silver before throwing them back in shame.

How can God abolish his own covenant? We have heard threats to this end before, but now it will be carried out. While not wiping out God's will to restore, it could be read as a statement of his authority to do what he pleases. The shepherds have been bad shepherds, they have misled the people and they have not been worthy or wise as leaders. But how could the people have consistently been so stupid? Is it because God has already abandoned them, so that they could not make wise choices? It's a complete double-bind.

We are caught up in further distressing confusion – the more distressing because we cannot harmonise such experience with our need to inhabit a moral universe. Is God's sovereignty greater that God's morality? Or have we misunderstood the ethical demands that accompany election and call? Do they apply to God's representatives but not to God?

All these, and more, are questions that are hard to avoid in any honest reading of these verses.

4 'Mindful triumph'?

Zechariah 12:1—13:1

Jerusalem is facing its final conflict, and the stakes are higher than those of power games between neighbours. The chief actor is 'the Lord who stretched out the heavens' (12:1), and the unfolding drama of divine victory is working out on a cosmic stage. Instead of the celebrations, though, we have an unexpected picture of the triumph scene. The people look on an unidentified victim and their response is not jubilation but mourning, as those who were responsible for the abuse are grief-stricken by its results. We are not told whether this was something from years long past or a result of more recent troubles, only that God has enabled a change in their fundamental disposition, towards compassion and mercy (12:10).

There is no unanimous view among scholars as to what precisely the prophet intends here, but since chapter divisions do not always mark the sense and flow of thought we might read on to the first verse of chapter 13. As we do this, we discover that the personal mourning of each group comes together 'on that day' with the release of a fountain of cleansing. What can we learn from a drama where, through looking at what they have done, and not turning away, people receive cleansing and redemption?

Often we come to understand a text by starting 'from within'. But if we have too few clues to come to a reasonable judgement about who or what it is talking about, we have to choose between ignoring it or interpreting it from another point of view, outside of its first, unknown, point of reference. If we choose the latter, we take a different sort of responsibility for our reading, but it need not just be a stab in the dark. Where might we go if we make a conscious choice to follow the trail of the gospel according to John? It seems, in John 19:37, that the author has picked up Zechariah 12:10 and used it in isolation as a proof text to describe a soldier piercing Jesus' side with a spear. But John's use of the phrase enables a seminal shift, from the soldier's wounding of Jesus and witnessing to his own act, to Jesus showing the disciples his hands *and his side* (John 20:20), as one of the physical signs of victimhood is displayed in the resurrected Christ.

5 No room for sham imitations

Just as we think we have come to a conclusion, the stage revolves again and it's not yet time for the curtain call. Those who returned from exile knew that return and resolution were not exactly the same thing. Idols and prophets are bracketed together; there is nothing good about either of them here. Although names were more significant in the ancient Near East then they usually are for us, they still carry meaning today. We are aware not only of how we are most personally and deeply affected by those whom we know directly, 'by name', but also that there are times when, by way of protest or objection, we attempt to 'depersonalise' some politicians by referring to them by their role rather than by name. To 'cut off the names of the idols from the land' (v. 2) is to ensure they will no longer hold any residual power to affect how people live.

More perplexing is the lambasting of the prophets: it is as if all prophecy from that time would be reckoned a sham, and no one who once owned the name of a prophet will admit to it now. Prophets have parted company with truth-telling. Their own parents will turn against them, and they themselves will go out of their way to avoid being associated with that role, claiming that their priority in life has always been the tending of family land and fabricating other reasons for scars which may have come from prophetic ecstasy (compare 1 Kings 18:28). The culture 'on that day', contrary to expectation, will be one of fear, of desperately trying to keep personal history away from the public gaze.

And there is worse: as God commands the sword to strike the shepherd, his co-worker (v. 7), we find that he fares no better than the 'worthless shepherd' of 11:17. This seems to be power gone mad, and it is being displayed by God himself. There is further tribulation for the sheep who are scattered without protection after the slaughter of the shepherd. Two-thirds of them will not survive, and the rest will be left to endure further suffering before they can call on the name of the Lord and be answered and recognised. The devastation leaves us reeling – all for the sake of the redemption of the few.

Do we have to be undergoing great distress and extreme suffering in order to fully comprehend such passages? Refusing to accept a balance of power between that which destroys and that which gives life, Zechariah leans towards later apocalyptic literature as he proclaims God's ultimate responsibility for everything.

6 No easy transformation

Zechariah 14

This last part of the book, like the first, ends with a promise of God's rule from an entirely secure Jerusalem. It is universal in its scope: there will be no choice (vv. 16–19). The culmination of history has arrived in all its terror and all its promise. Jerusalem is defeated by an onslaught from 'all the nations', but in the wake of this God brings a seismic shift to the whole landscape. He stands on the Mount of Olives and the weight of his presence splits it in two – no natural barrier or protection is now needed for the city. In a dramatic reversal, God's rule will be irrefutable. Those who have waged war against Jerusalem will be afflicted with terrible plague, strong bodies will rot away and relationships of allies will crumble into mutual destruction (vv. 12–13). Now, and only now, will Jerusalem be the centre of light and life, united in God's service. Everyone and everything serves his good purpose; there is no difference between the ordinary cooking pots and the precious bowls made for temple ritual (v. 20).

Zechariah 14 has strong significance for both Jewish and Christian readers. For Jewish congregations, it is one of the texts of the haftarah, a collection of passages from the prophets for sabbath and festival readings, and is recited on the first day of Sukkot. This festival looks back to the years of dwelling in temporary accommodation in the wilderness, recognising both the vulnerability of life and the blessing of God's protection. Verse 16 commands the keeping of the festival by all the families of the earth. The establishing of a permanent dwelling in the everlasting city and God's kingship over all the earth constituted there are, some would say, signs of an inward and lasting transformation.

In Christian reading, the author of the book of Revelation will keep company with and yet go further than this prophet, when he proclaims a new Jerusalem as a place of unsurpassed blessing and the dwelling place of the redeemed. There are also tantalising specific allusions drawn up into Christian testimony, such as Jesus speaking of the removal of 'this mountain' in Mark 11:23 and the narrative of his ascension from the Mount of Olives. All things come together. When there seems no human way out, the apocalyptic texts bear witness that the way to stay human is to acknowledge that God's horizons are immeasurably wider than the present.

Guidelines

- The image of the ruler of God's people is seen as both triumphant and humble (9:9), and the gospels according to Matthew and John find this a reference to the messianic entrance of Jesus into Jerusalem (Mathew 21; John 12). While many contemporary worship songs reflect the warrior aspect of the Saviour, our Christian reading-glasses usually make for a readier focus on his humility. Does the phrase 'triumphant and victorious' slip quietly away behind 'humble and riding on a donkey'? How does he help us to hold power and humility together?

- Zechariah sharpens our perception that powerful leaders rarely fall without damaging those who have followed their leadership, and reinforces a sense of coming disaster wherever leaders abrogate their vocation as godly and compassionate shepherds (chapters 10—11). How might he speak to those under extreme duress today?

- As we read about cosmic battles, awesome in the scale of their destruction, we may well agree with the criticism of those who find our faith unpalatable and of many who share it, who ask how we can act as if there is no problem believing in a God who acts in such a way. From J.R.R. Tolkien to C.S. Lewis, through to the avowedly anti-religious stance of Philip Pullman, a range of novelists have invited us within a cosmic battleground without becoming warmongers in the process. Why do we find it so difficult to enter the deep myths and stories of scripture in the same way?

- Go back to 12:10 and ask yourself who is, or who are, the wounded victim(s) in our times? How are we asked to look on them and not turn away, and have our dispositions changed?

FURTHER READING

Joyce G. Baldwin, *Haggai, Zechariah and Malachi: An introduction and commentary (Tyndale Old Testament Commentaries)*, vol. 28 (InterVarsity Press, 1972).

Michael Fishbane, *The JPS Bible Commentary: Haftarot* (JPS, 2002).

Andrew Knowles, *The Bible Guide* (Augsburg, 2001).

C.L. Meyers and E.M. Meyers, *Haggai, Zechariah 1–8: A new translation with introduction and commentary (Anchor Bible Commentary)* (Doubleday, 1987).

Julia M. O'Brien, *Nahum, Habakkuk, Zephaniah, Haggai, Zechariah, Malachi (Abingdon Old Testament Commentaries)* (Abingdon Press 2004).

2 Samuel: politics human and divine

David G. Firth

For many, David is the hero of the Old Testament. Coming from 1 Samuel, we might think this is reasonable – provided we are untroubled by him working for the Philistines. But the David who emerges in 2 Samuel is a more complex and disturbing figure. He can be gracious – lamenting Saul and Jonathan's deaths. He can be grasping – taking Uriah's wife and issuing a chilling order for his death. He is consumed by grief when his son Absalom dies, but seemingly unmoved by his daughter Tamar's rape. He reflects profoundly on the nature of his rule in his 'last words' (23:1–7), yet he pleads powerlessness when it suits (3:31–39). What unites these elements is that David is engaged in politics, and politics is complicated. Politics involves dealing with people we might rather avoid, making decisions that are not necessarily right or wrong, but simply the best that can be managed. David was not separate from the politics of his time and its complexity as different groups sought control of Israel, with pressures coming from outsiders, like the Philistines, from Israelites who aligned themselves with Saul's family or even from within David's family. David made imperfect choices because he was imperfect and the world in which he lived was imperfect.

Rather than seeing David as the hero, it would be better to look to God. He is at least a more reliable figure in Samuel, though being reliable does not mean he steps in to prevent bad choices humans make. David's murder of Uriah was 'evil in the eyes of Yahweh', but he did not prevent it. Tamar's rape is part of his punishment of David's house. God lets humans make their choices, with all their frequently gruesome implications. But God doesn't stay out of politics. He establishes a covenant with David (chapter 7) that is crucial for the whole of the Old Testament. For all David's flaws, God chooses to work with and through him. In Samuel we are reminded that in a sinful world, even God's politics involves dealing with those who are less than desirable to achieve the best possible outcome, even if that is far from good, because through this God's purposes are still being worked out.

Unless otherwise stated, Bible quotations are taken from the ESV or are my own translation.

1 David hears of Saul and Jonathan's deaths

2 Samuel 1

Although we divide the books of Samuel, they are really one continuous story. This chapter opens immediately after the deaths of Saul and his sons on Mount Gilboa (1 Samuel 31). Because the Philistines had sent him away (1 Samuel 29), David was as far as was possible from those events. It took three days before an Amalekite arrived with news of their death. In questioning him, David drew out an account at some variance from the previous chapter, suggesting that the Amalekite was not a disinterested figure; all the more so when he produced Saul's badges of rank after admitting he had killed Saul. The Amalekite described this as a mercy killing; but David had twice refused to kill Saul (1 Samuel 24, 26). The Amalekite seemed to assume he would be rewarded by David for giving him this news, since he was careful to present himself in the best possible light. Instead, having confirmed he was subject to Israel's law as a resident foreigner, David ordered his execution. His reason was that the Amalekite had destroyed Yahweh's anointed.

Might David have taken a more lenient approach? Possibly, but killing a king under any circumstances sets a dangerous precedent, and David would not want to be associated with that if he allowed the man to live. Politically, it was necessary that he should not claim the throne through someone who had killed the king. In any case, the man had confessed to murder, however much he might present it positively. But David was not solely driven by politics, and his lament over Saul and Jonathan represents a profound insight into his grief. As an especially close friend, Jonathan perhaps comes over more positively, but David still grieved over Saul. Sometimes, doing the right thing and doing what is politically astute comes together. But sometimes it is also important not only to do the right thing, but that this be seen too. This need not mean everything is done for show, for then words become empty. But where we have made better choices and others can learn from them, it is still appropriate to make them known.

2 Two kingdoms arise

2 Samuel 2:1–11

God was never said to act in the previous chapter. That lack is remedied here, but we still see God dealing with human politics. David had not enquired of God in executing the Amalekite, perhaps because the law was clear. But David was confronted by new circumstances. Saul was dead, and God had promised that David would be king (1 Samuel 16:1–13). David had refused to grasp the throne, so how would he now become king? David needed God to guide him. These enquiries seem to assume he had access to the Urim and Thummim, stones through which God gave specific guidance via a priest. Thus guided, David went to Hebron, a major city in Judah's far south closely associated with him. He did not go alone – he took his family and men – and there the men of Judah anointed him as their king.

David was king of one tribe, but Saul had been king of the whole country. Support from Judah was not unexpected (David had built a following there), but the promise was that he would be king of all Israel. The move to Hebron was led by God, but in reaching out to the people of Jabesh-gilead, David was contacting a northern town which had been loyal to Saul (1 Samuel 11:1–11; 31:11–13). God had provided David with a power base in the south, but David also had to deal with potential adversaries if he was to bring the nation together. His language is careful, encouraging them to see that shared faith was crucial, even as he invited them to join him.

But other adversaries were not yet convinced, and Abner installed Saul's son Ish-bosheth as king. Nominally, Ish-bosheth claimed all the north, though in reality it was a smaller area. David's actions in this passage are all appropriate – depending on God and also encouraging others to see what God is doing. But his adversaries still opposed him. A longer-term view of events is needed, one that insists on a politics that conforms to God's purposes, but which looks beyond the short term – indeed, David would be based in Hebron for more than seven years.

3 Two kingdoms go to war

Two kings claiming the one land is a recipe for conflict. That conflict emerged as Abner led Ish-bosheth's forces to Gibeon, a strategic site north of Judah that controlled access to the coast. The details are unclear, but it seems some representative combat did not resolve things. Subsequently, Abner's forces were defeated by David's, though the battle was fierce. We quickly see that the political becomes the personal, as the battle between the two kings' forces is focused on the conflict between David's leaders (Joab, Abishai and Asahel) and Ish-bosheth's commander (Abner). In particular, Joab's brother Asahel chased Abner. Although Abner tried to discourage Asahel, he eventually killed him, even though he knew this would trigger a feud with Joab. When some Benjaminites joined him, Abner addressed Joab, leading to a cessation of conflict. Has detente emerged now that Joab no longer pursued Abner's forces?

As is often the case in civil wars, cessation of these initial skirmishes does not end the conflict, even though the casualty count shows that David's forces were more effective. Asahel could be buried, and Joab took his forces back to Hebron. But the war did not end. Rather, it continued for some time, even if David's house gradually became more powerful than Saul's. This growing strength is evidenced by David's marriages and children, pointing to a range of alliances, some internal to Israel and some with minor kingdoms nearby. David had declined to fight Saul himself, but now he has been drawn into battle with Saul's family. His marriages show a willingness to employ the patterns of power that typified his world, a hint that David might be willing to claim the throne of all Israel by force. Yet mention of Abigail in his list of wives also points to another time when David contemplated using violence to achieve his own ends (1 Samuel 25). Even when God is not mentioned – and he barely features in this account – 2 Samuel is careful to hint at alternatives to violence, even in a world that assumes this is the appropriate way to deal with opposition.

4 Kings and strongmen

Civil wars are not only fought between rulers – military strongmen often see them as a chance to advance their own position. Added to this, the greatest danger to a king often came from those around him. So, in a conflict between the houses of Saul and David, it is not surprising that Abner was making himself more powerful. But would he have had a sexual relationship with Saul's secondary wife Rizpah? The text does not tell us if Ish-bosheth is paranoid or confronting Abner for a clear wrong. What matters is that Abner is determined to transfer the kingdom to David, claiming it was what Yahweh had sworn to him. Did Abner know about David's anointing, or is he making a political assessment? Either way, he was soon meeting with David, though only after arranging for David's first wife, Michal, to be returned to him. He also met with Israel's elders and insisted that Yahweh had promised to save his people from the Philistines through David. We have no recorded prophetic saying that matches this; it seems Abner is summing up what he sees Yahweh doing as a means of persuading others. Through this, Abner reported to David that he could bring the support of the north.

Abner was the northern strongman, but Joab had that role in the south, and although Abner had left David in peace, Joab was not content. Instead, he caught up with Abner and on the pretext of speaking privately, murdered him. Joab's claim that this was because Abner was deceiving David rings hollow, especially as the wound he gave Abner exactly matches the one Abner had given to Asahel (2:23). David denied any involvement in Abner's death, lamenting for him as he had earlier done for Saul and Jonathan (1:17–27), while adding a curse on Joab and his house. Everyone here ends up twisting faith in Yahweh to develop their own political ends. It is still an easy thing to do, but it is as ugly now as it was then.

5 The throne comes to David

Abner's death meant that David could not seize the throne or have it seized for him. But others were prepared to use violence to bring the whole kingdom to David. This possibility became greater because Ish-bosheth's position was not strong – Abner was the power behind his throne, and, without him, Ish-bosheth's support diminished rapidly. While resting at home, he was murdered by two of his bodyguard, who took his head to David at Hebron that night. As this journey was more than 60 miles, it shows their urgency. When they met David, they too tried to claim that God had been at work, asserting that Yahweh had avenged David on Saul and his family. Since Jonathan's son Mephibosheth was still alive, we know that part of their claim was false, and the one thing David had been careful to avoid was unnecessary conflict with Saul's family. Hence, David saw through their claim, placing them in the same position as the Amalekite who had reported Saul's death (1:1–16), and ordering their execution since they had admitted to murder.

It would be nice to think that David's final accession to the throne was separate from this, but it was after Ish-bosheth's death that the northern tribes came to David in Hebron to acknowledge him as king. David had recognised that he could not seize the throne, and he avoided that temptation. But in the messiness of Israel's politics, he was still acknowledged as king. The northern tribes claimed that their move was because of Yahweh's promise, though it is likely that they (like Abner) had discerned Yahweh's leading rather than citing an earlier promise. David was finally king as Yahweh had promised, and he established it on a just basis by formalising a covenant with the tribes. Yahweh thus brought his king to the throne of the nation, but he did it by working through convoluted human politics. Amid human grasping and violence, God is pointing to an alternative, but it is an alternative seen only because of the darkness to which the human drive for power leads us.

6 God grants the victories

God's king is finally reigning over God's people. As readers, we know this because we have been given information not available to those about whom we read. But, given the political complications that have shaped everything to this point, can anyone know that this is indeed God's purposes being worked out? Or could this simply be a case of the winners claiming that God is on their side?

These two passages provide the outer boundaries of a compressed version of the whole of David's reign, demonstrating that Yahweh was indeed with David, despite his weaknesses. In particular, they demonstrate that God's presence could be seen in tangible ways and they are marked by repetition of the fact that Yahweh was with David (5:10, 12) and that David won battles because Yahweh gave him victory (5:20, 25; 8:6, 14). It is notable that these statements about God's presence with David are presented as testimony both to David and also to the wider readership of Samuel, so all see how God was working through David. The politics that brought Israel to this point were murky, with plenty of unsavoury characters involved. And one of them, Joab, continued to be involved as David took Jerusalem. The complexities of dealing with real people are not removed simply because we are involved in God's purposes.

That David is Yahweh's chosen king does not mean the task of governing is necessarily straightforward. David needed to be an astute politician and commander, and it is through this that we see Yahweh working. Taking Jerusalem and making it his capital was politically astute, as Jerusalem was not held by any tribe and sat on the border of the northern and southern tribes. Developing relationships with states on Israel's boundaries, such as Tyre, laid positive foundations for Israel's future. Defeating the Philistines (5:17–25) and the various minor states around Israel (8:1–14) created a context where Israel could thrive. All of this could only be achieved because of what Yahweh was doing, but along with this David still had to ensure justice within Israel. Thus, all could know they had God's chosen king.

Guidelines

We live in a world where politics and violence, especially but not only in warfare, mark the lives of many people. One of the great emphases of the Bible is that God's goal is to bring his people to a world that is marked by wholeness and peace (see, for example, Isaiah 65:17–25). That is where God is ultimately taking us in Jesus, and indeed one of the great themes of Jesus' death is that he has taken the worst of our violence on to himself and defeated it in the resurrection. This is a crucial point for us to remember in terms of God's ultimate purposes.

But 2 Samuel is not primarily about those ultimate purposes. Rather, it is a book that engages with the real world as Israel encountered it. David became king of Israel not by God avoiding human politics and its frequent propensity for violence, but rather by God interacting with this world as it was. We should not think everything David did in these chapters was blessed by God; but we can certainly see God making the best of a sinful world here. We might prefer a world where only good choices can be made, but that is not yet this world. If God is to interact with this world, that involves him working in and through the complexity of human politics. Sometimes, that politics is very messy (e.g. Ish-bosheth's murder) and involves dealing with people who are less than savoury (who, after all, would want to cross Joab?). Other points, such as David defeating the Philistines, clearly produced a good outcome for Israel, but still meant dealing with complex political realities and their implications.

As we reflect on these chapters, it should lead us to pray for Christians involved in politics today. The challenges they face will vary depending on the level at which they operate, but the types of choices they have to make will be similar – they will need to make the best of situations in which no one choice can be described as good. Indeed, if there was only a 'good' option, then it would not represent much of a challenge. But Christians in politics face struggles to allocate limited budgets, conflicting opinions on what is best in a given circumstance and, at upper levels, questions of when force might be used. But this is a world in which God continues to be active, and we can pray for him to lead those involved in making these choices.

1 Worship at the centre

2 Samuel 6; 22:47–51

David achieved important political successes. But this was not central to kingship in Israel; rather, they were to lead the nation into a deeper relationship with Yahweh.

Today's readings are separated by the long story of David's sin and its consequences. But they are bound together within Samuel's structure as central components of segments reflecting the whole of David's reign. Together, they show what is expected of the king. In 2 Samuel 6, David takes the ark of the covenant, left aside for much of Saul's reign, and brings it to the city of David, that part of Jerusalem designated as the royal centre. This is something a king of that time might be expected to do, bringing a marker of divine presence to himself. But David's arrangements were haphazard, ignoring the requirements for moving the ark (Numbers 4:1–16) and moving it as the Philistines had done earlier (1 Samuel 6:1–16). David's desire to worship and bring the ark was probably genuine, but he was also supposed to ensure the law was kept. A genuine desire to honour Yahweh does not mean his motives were pure – his concern was bringing the ark to himself. Only when he saw the blessing it brought did he bring it properly.

Uzzah's death shows the tragedy of right motives for wrong acts. When David brought the ark properly, he could rejoice, even if it meant showing the king as lead worshipper, not someone of inherent power. Michal had not grasped this. As king, David reigned before Yahweh, not for self-aggrandisement. This same theme runs through David's song in 2 Samuel 22, a response to Yahweh giving him rest, and probably from a time earlier than in 2 Samuel 6. In it, David expresses a core insight that he did not always live up to: it is Yahweh who provides security, who gives victory. Thus, David could vow to praise Yahweh among the nations (2 Samuel 22:50), knowing that his role was to proclaim the God who gives victory. For God's king, practising God's politics is not about claiming power for oneself; rather, it is leading all in faithful praise to the nations.

2 An eternal promise

David lived in his house, and Yahweh had given him rest. It is something every king wanted. But ancient kings typically showed their commitment through building temples that honoured their gods. With the ark in Jerusalem, doing this made sense, especially as the ark was in a temporary dwelling while David dwelt in a house panelled with cedar. Building a temple (literally a 'house') seemed so obvious that when David suggested it to Nathan, the prophet simply told him to do so because Yahweh was with him.

But not everything a prophet says is from God. And, that night Yahweh spoke to Nathan to make clear that David would not build him a house – but he would build one for David. This passage is central to much of the Old Testament, especially for the messianic hope. Above all, Yahweh demonstrated that the proper order for politics within Israel was that Yahweh established what mattered, not the king. The house that mattered was not somewhere for the ark; the house that mattered was a royal dynasty in which the king was subject to Yahweh. David only became king because Yahweh chose him, and when his descendants ruled it would be on Yahweh's terms. David appreciated this in his prayer, understanding that it must be Yahweh's name that is magnified forever.

Much of the story that follows shows David in a rather different light, but in his 'last words' in chapter 23 we encounter an old David who has learned some hard lessons. Here, he passes on the key insight to all who rule (not only kings): the leadership which delivers justice before God is the one where God's blessing is experienced. David by then knew that he could not claim to have done this, but because of the promise of God, he knew his house was in this position. This promise will have its highs and lows along the way, but it finally reaches Jesus. In noting this, we do not lose sight of the fact that all politics among the people of God are challenged to see leadership in how God is honoured, not in projects that attain glory for ourselves.

3 Loyalty and conflict

2 Samuel 9—10

Although these stories are distinct, both focus on David acting loyally towards others. The term used is sometimes translated 'kindness', but 'loyalty' is probably better. David had promised Jonathan that he would care for his family (1 Samuel 20:42). The decline of Saul's family meant he could have removed them completely; instead, David remembered his commitment to Jonathan. We have already learned of Mephibosheth and the accident that left him lame (4:4). As Saul's descendant, Mephibosheth might still be perceived as a threat. But having discovered his whereabouts through a former member of Saul's staff (Ziba), David arranged for Mephibosheth to come to court and receive the family estate. Loyalty had to transcend the threat of a potential rival.

By contrast, David's attempt to demonstrate loyalty towards the Ammonite king Hanun is less well received. We do not know what David's previous relationship with Nahash was; perhaps they were just both enemies of Saul (compare 1 Samuel 11:1–11). Whatever the background, David's loyalty was sharply rebuffed; Hanun's advisors suggested that David had sent spies, not comforters. Their decision to shame David's messengers triggered a war that is not resolved until 2 Samuel 12:26–31. The reports here are of only a part of the war, showing the interaction between the personal and the political that was so much a part of the ancient world (as indeed ours). Joab looks surprisingly positive here, though this is part of a series of character reversals that run through the account of this war, in which a Hittite will be the most loyal of all Yahweh's servants. By the end of chapter 10, Israel is at peace with Aram, but not Ammon.

In some ways, these chapters prepare readers for events about to be reported. But together, they also reflect on what loyalty looks like. They encourage loyalty that respects promises made before, even though doing so is potentially costly. Practising loyalty does not guarantee desirable outcomes, because faith does not remove the reality of politics. Showing loyalty is not done for a reward; it is done because this is how God's people are meant to live.

4 Evil in the eyes of the Lord

2 Samuel 11

This is one of the best-known stories about David, and also the most devastating. This is the ugly David we would rather not see. Although David is as close as the book of Samuel comes to a human hero, it is unflinching in showing his capacity for evil.

The war begun in the previous chapter was still raging. In spring, when weather and farming needs made it easier to do so, David sent Joab and the army back, besieging the Ammonite capital, Rabbah. David, however, remained in Jerusalem. Is this problematic? Since 2 Samuel 10 showed Israel winning battles without David, it need not have been. It is what David did while there that is troubling.

Walking on the palace roof, he saw a woman bathing, probably using a bowl while lightly dressed. David was interested and sent to find out about her, discovering her name and that of her family and husband. Knowing Bathsheba was married, he still sent and had her brought. Nothing here suggests any active involvement on Bathsheba's part: David is always the active one. But she became pregnant. As a result, Joab had to send back her husband. Despite David's blandishments, Uriah the Hittite would not sleep with his wife, understanding what was expected from Israel, even though his own heritage was Canaanite. Even drunk, Uriah was more upright than a sober David. Finally, showing the loyalty David no longer does, he carried the message that ordered his own execution. Joab was astute enough to know that David's plan for killing Uriah would be too obviously murder and so modified the plan, even though many died as a result. Eventually, David took Uriah's wife as his own, though we are not told what Bathsheba thought.

Only in the chapter's last line is Yahweh mentioned, but the statement is important – David's actions were not secret, because Yahweh had seen. No one is exempt from Yahweh's rule; those in power may not claim God's support simply because of their position. God's people may be tempted to follow the models of politics seen around us, but that God sees even what is done in secret suggests there is always an alternative that is demanded.

5 The sword shall never depart

David's actions were evil. But he was God's chosen king. How would these elements balance out? In part, anyone who has read Hannah's prayer (1 Samuel 2:1–10) knows Yahweh opposes those who use power for their own ends. Although God does not intervene in every case of evil (human freedom remains important), this time God's commitment to justice among his people demanded action. This happened as Nathan presented David with a story about a rich man abusing the poor. It is crucial that David both understood and misunderstood. He had to understand, because such acts were unacceptable; but he had to misunderstand, because it was really a story about him. Only when David condemned the rich man could Nathan spring the trap, declaring, 'You are the man!' In spite of all Yahweh had given him, he had struck down Uriah and taken his wife. David's declaration against the rich man was used by Yahweh when announcing David's punishment. What David had done secretly, Yahweh would do in public. At this point, we see a key difference between David and Saul – where Saul had resisted Yahweh's punishment, David accepted it. There was still a penalty – the child does die – but David would not himself be put to death. Even so, David still hoped for grace (confusing his staff by mourning when his child was born), but finally accepted this. God's politics do not tolerate kings abusing his people.

But failure is not where the story ends. After the child's death, David and Bathsheba had another child, Solomon. But Yahweh called him Jedidiah, or 'beloved of Yahweh'. The circumstances of this birth were hardly promising, but God's grace is seen at this point. This is not because David merited anything – it is not grace if it is merited – but because Yahweh chose to work with a king who for all his failures understood that human authority is valid only when submitted to God's. As this chapter ends, it not only closes off the account of the war, but it also points to the continued possibility of David's reign as a now chastened king, one who understood that the final authority among God's people is always God's alone.

6 A family in conflict

2 Samuel 13

In confronting David over his sin with Uriah and Bathsheba, Nathan insisted that 'the sword shall never depart from your house' (12:10). David had employed sexual and military violence to attack others, and now he experienced that in his own family. We should also note the resonances of the word 'house', picking up on Yahweh's promise from 2 Samuel 7 that he would build a house for David. In effect, Yahweh allowed the forces David had unleashed to work themselves out in his house so David felt in his own person the effects of his own sin on others. Nevertheless, in all the gruesome events of this chapter, it is never said that Yahweh brought them about. Indeed, God is never mentioned within it. Humans who are playing their own power games are perfectly capable of inflicting the sort of violence of which Nathan had spoken.

Along with the more obvious and grotesque forms of violence, this chapter also points to the ways people manipulate one another to achieve their ends. Jonadab was a shrewd advisor, but he was content to work the system, bringing Amnon together with his sister Tamar for something he must have known was entirely inappropriate. Perhaps he could not have predicted the actual turn of events – though since he could read Amnon's purposes well enough, maybe he could have known. Amnon manipulated even his own feelings of love and hate in raping his sister. Absalom seemingly offered Tamar security, but appears to do nothing but plot his own revenge. Amnon and Absalom both treated their servants dismissively. David was manipulated by all and was at various points angry, longing, and ultimately comforted over Amnon, but otherwise puzzlingly inert. He could have acted with justice to prevent many of the events described here, but he did not act. Through all of this, Tamar is treated as a pawn in everyone's power games, so that even the special robe she wore as a member of the royal family seemed to mock her. What we are seeing here is the wages of sin working themselves out. It is a chapter that is full of ugliness, which is precisely what sin is.

Guidelines

Newspaper headlines (or at least some of them) often express themselves in dualistic terms – someone is either good or bad. This is especially the case with more notorious criminals, though there is always a particular interest in Christian leaders who fail and the resultant accusations of hypocrisy. But only those who stay out of the complexities of human relationships have the luxury of seeing the world in those terms. The rest of us have to deal with people who are a mix of good and bad.

The David we encounter in these chapters is just this sort of mixture. In bringing the ark to Jerusalem and looking to establish a temple, he shows a clear appreciation of what was central to Israel's life. And in accepting that Yahweh was the one who would choose if and when a temple was to be built, he shows that an Israelite king always reigned under God – it was not for the king to decide what should be done and retrospectively ask God to bless it. His songs in the Samuel conclusion also reflect on this. In all this, he is someone we might want to emulate. This is especially the case for those of us called to Christian leadership, since the desire to make our own decisions and then expect God to approve them remains a constant temptation. Of course, sometimes acting positively and graciously towards someone can be misconstrued (as by Hanun), but this is still the right way to act.

But David did not always act in a way that we should emulate. He might have sometimes shown real insight, but, as we have seen, he also demonstrated a profound ability to become the problem. It was David who unleashed the forces of violence by his own abuse of others. He was the one through whom God was prepared to work, but he was very far from perfect. In this, the Bible is prepared to show us a realistic David and to accept that God worked through very imperfect people. Indeed, though he was far from perfect, the promise to David is the foundation of the messianic hope in the Old Testament that brings us to Jesus. All this should make us realise that our focus is therefore not so much on individuals like David. Rather, we look to God as the one who brings real change in a world where everyone is a mix of good and bad.

1 Power plays

2 Samuel 14:1—15:12

In 1 Samuel, Eli's sons had brought him trouble (1 Samuel 1—2), and Samuel's sons had likewise caused him problems (1 Samuel 8:1–5). Within Samuel, it is unsurprising that David's sons do the same. Unlike the others, David's problems are expressly working out the effects of sin, showing how violence begets violence. All this progressively makes evident that what David had tried to do in private now expresses itself publicly. We might want sin to be private, but it has a habit of becoming public.

The complication here is that Joab recognised David's desire for Absalom to return, and so he brought in a wise woman to convince David to do so. Joab attempted to replicate Nathan's technique, as the story he gave the woman also initially looks like a legal matter. But David wouldn't be fooled again, his question quickly making clear that he saw through Joab's attempt to manipulate him. But he seemed also to believe the goal of this was appropriate, and so he arranged for Absalom's return. Yet he refused to see his son. As manipulative as ever, Absalom decided to force Joab's hand to bring him back to his father. But when they met, there was no warmth. There was too much suspicion for that.

If Absalom could manipulate Joab, we ought not be surprised he also manipulated the political and judicial systems. The king appears to have functioned as the final court of appeal. Absalom took advantage of this and presented himself to all as the one who would give justice – like an opposition figure who promises everyone what they want. The reality of delivering justice is more complex, but it was enough for Absalom to return to his hometown of Hebron and launch a coup. There must have been genuine dissatisfaction with David, perhaps hinted at as Absalom was joined by Ahithophel (possibly Bathsheba's grandfather).

This is a story of human scheming and manipulation, of half-truths and ambition. David remains as inert as the previous chapter, seemingly rendered impotent by his sin. As a result, the whole nation suffers – and things are about to get worse. But that is what sin does.

2 Changing perspectives

Careful readers may have noted that God has barely been mentioned since Nathan's encounter with David, and only by those who sought to use God for their own purposes. But now, as David fled from Absalom by heading towards the Jordan via the Mount of Olives, we begin to see subtle reminders of God's presence and that God will ultimately bring a chastened David back to Jerusalem.

Initially, David's flight seems like an expression of panic, though he still had some who are loyal. But there was a semblance of order as some troops marched past. Remarkably, it was one of them, Ittai the Gittite, who began to reshape David's view of events. As a Gittite, he was a foreigner from the Philistine city of Gath. There is a contrast here with 1 Samuel 17. There, while encountering Goliath (also from Gath), David reshaped Saul's' view of events to see what God was doing. Ittai's brief words of encouragement were followed by others, including those who brought the ark with them. But David was learning and, unlike Israel in 1 Samuel 4—6, did not presume God's support, returning it to Jerusalem. And at the top of the mountain, David prayed for the first time in this conflict (15:31). It was a brief prayer that represents a turning point, as he then met Hushai the Archite. Like Uriah, he was a descendant of the surviving Canaanites, but he committed himself to serving David by being his agent in Absalom's court. Prayer and wisdom here combine as God works through unexpected people.

David's subsequent encounters with Ziba and then Shimei in chapter 16 show that he still faced widespread opposition. Even in this, he was still learning, so when Abishai offered to kill Shimei for him, David recognised (as he had with Saul; 1 Samuel 26:8–11) that violence by proxy was still not the way forward. This is not David as the model king, and within Samuel he never really is again. But this is David learning what is expected from a king in Israel through foreigners who can teach him about God and prayer.

3 Advisors collide

David's brief prayer continues to lie in the background as events unfold here, and God continues to work through surprising people. Hushai had arrived in Jerusalem at the same time as Absalom (15:37). Leaving David's flight to one side, the narrative focuses on Hushai's encounter with Absalom as he convinced Absalom to allow him to serve in his court. Absalom was naturally suspicious, and Hushai had to be careful in his speech – almost everything he said must be heard as supporting Absalom while in reality supporting David. But he was still a secondary advisor; Ahithophel was the one to whom Absalom turned. His advice involved sexual violence directed against the concubines David left behind, though within their culture that would have been understood as attacking David. From Absalom's perspective, that was the main goal – publicly raping these women apparently was not a problem. In case we miss the cultural nuances, we are assured that getting advice from Ahithophel was considered to be as good as getting it directly from God.

Ahithophel's status shows the problem Hushai faced. How could he serve David? The answer is provided by some more advice from Ahithophel, where he proposed a sudden attack on David. Everyone was apparently persuaded, and yet Absalom decided to summon Hushai. Again, Hushai had to be careful, and though he declared that Ahithophel's counsel was 'not good', there was little of military value in his alternative proposal. Yet Absalom was persuaded. We are meant to be astonished by this, which is why we are told Yahweh had commanded the defeat of Ahithophel's advice to thwart Absalom. Hushai then used his networks to advise David so they could cross the Jordan. Ahithophel, by contrast, realising he had become disposable to Absalom and could never again serve David, committed suicide. David's prayer had been answered, even if only at the point where it seemed impossible. Absalom now led his men in what was effectively Ahithophel's plan, but the moment was lost. By contrast, others rallied around David and provided food and drink. One short prayer had changed everything, though it did not thereby undo the damage done by sin.

4 The battle of the forest

2 Samuel 18:1—19:8

David was king, but he was also a father, and it is clear that he struggled to separate these roles. As king, he needed to see the land restored to order. But as a father, he did not want to see Absalom suffer. Like many parents, his children caused him pain, but this did not stop him loving them. In some contexts, this is important and appropriate, but as king, David's relationship with them was different. This was especially the case with Absalom, since Absalom's rebellion harmed the whole nation. Although concern for Absalom was not why the army discouraged him from joining the battle, his instructions to his commanders show that this was his primary concern.

The battle report is brief, though telling. In noting that the forest killed more than David's forces, we see another hint that David's prayer was guiding matters, turning Ahithophel's advice to foolishness as David's men overcame Absalom's. The forest also played a decisive role in Absalom's own death, as he was caught in an oak. But here we see Joab's usual ruthlessness as he arranged Absalom's death. Only then is the battle finished.

The account of the messengers coming to David might seem odd. Why would Joab want a Cushite reporting Absalom's death rather than Ahimaaz? Perhaps he thought the Cushite was expendable – after all, David executed two others who reported royal deaths. As it happens, the Cushite was an astute messenger as it became clear that Absalom remained David's main concern. Absalom's death saw David paralysed by grief, something only altered when Joab confronted him before he resumed his place.

David's position was painful, but it was still the result of the violence he himself had unleashed. The victory over Absalom was not as he wanted, but it was an answer to his earlier prayer as Ahithophel's good advice was turned to foolishness. This was a messy world where answers to prayer were also messy. And when God interacts with our politics, he still engages with a world like this. Prayer remains vital, but it does not remove us from the painful implications of our earlier choices.

5 David's return and another rebellion

Can what is broken be reassembled? Perhaps. But anyone looking closely will still see the fractures. This reality is evident as David was returning to Jerusalem. Absalom was defeated, and the nation could come back together, but not as it once was. Once unleashed, violence continues to find expression even if various processes might limit it to some extent.

The possibility of restoration emerged as David headed to the Jordan on his way to Jerusalem. As he journeyed, he met various people he had encountered while fleeing from Absalom, plus a few extras (like Mephibosheth). David's primary goal in these encounters was reconciliation, recognising that as king he needed to integrate his supporters with his enemies. This included again stopping a proposed execution of Shimei – though his deathbed instructions to Solomon might make us wonder about this (1 Kings 2:8–9). Likewise, simply splitting Saul's estate between Ziba and Mephibosheth looks like he lacked information to decide who had told the truth – though the book never tells us who did! The important point is that David had learnt that the king's task was to bring people together, not to create divisions, even when it was not his preferred option.

This approach initially appeared to pay dividends, as many joined him on his way. But old divisions also reappeared, and the damage David had initiated expressed itself in a second rebellion, this time led by Sheba (see chapter 20). Although David initially feared this rebellion would be as damaging as Absalom's, this one was more quickly resolved. But it is clear that some of David's attempted reconciliatory acts (such as Amasa commanding the army) were unable to stay, as Joab was as ruthless as ever. The closing notes of chapter 20 suggest that government structure was restored, and in a sense it was. Yet it was government deeply marked by the outcome of David's choices, one where violence remained an enduring issue. Restoration was possible and progress remained. But David's sin had affected the whole nation, and deep fractures remained. Not all sin will so self-evidently show the fractures left behind, but the reality is that they can still be seen in many churches today.

6 Two plague stories

Within 2 Samuel, both 5:17—8:14 and chapters 21—24 provide a summary of David's entire reign. Where the first summary is concerned with David's public acts, the second is more concerned with the private David, an individual dealing with implications of his own failures. Even the warrior accounts (21:15–22; 23:8–39) focus more on the achievements of David's men; however effective David was as a military leader, he needed good people with him.

The two passages we consider today are joined in various ways, especially as both demonstrate the problems kings can generate for their people. A king could bring justice to the nation, but a king who forgot the primacy of Yahweh's authority brought harm to the nation. This was true of both Saul and David, though only David saw the need for repentance in addressing this. As is typical of Samuel, it demonstrates that even when sin is addressed, this does not remove its implications. A king's sin is, however, more damaging because it affects so many more people.

The first account reports a famine because Saul had broken a covenant made with the Gibeonites, one of the remaining Canaanite groups (Joshua 9). David discovered this by seeking Yahweh, and began a process of reconciliation with them. However, it seems that he sought also to gain some advantage over Saul's family, and only after he accepted Rizpah's principled resistance did the famine end. The second account is more complex, but here it seems that David sought to use Yahweh's command to his own advantage in developing the army. Like Saul, David's using kingship to his own advantage was unacceptable, and this triggered a plague that was only stopped when Yahweh relented. David at least realised the importance of this, and ensured his worship was personally costly – as king he could have accepted Araunah's offer, but that would perpetuate the problem. Hence, we see the dangers and the possibilities for leaders among God's people – leadership that becomes self-serving damages the people as a whole, and this damage is not easily removed. But leaders who understand this can renew their people's relationship with God.

58

Guidelines

At the heart of the gospel is forgiveness, the reality that in Jesus Christ we can be forgiven and live a new life in the power of the Spirit. But the need for forgiveness points to the reality of sin. When we are forgiven, we know the joy of being restored in our relationship with God. While being forgiven means that sin's ultimate implication is addressed, it does not mean that sin's other implications are removed. Believers are forgiven in Christ, but that does not mean that the effects of our sin on others are removed. Indeed, sin has the unfortunate effect of damaging those around us. We might think sin is something private, but actually that sin will often impact others in unanticipated ways.

Throughout the chapters we have been reading this week, we encountered the reality of sin and its effects on others. This is particularly evident in the rebellions of Absalom and Sheba, both of which can in various ways be traced back to David's sin against Uriah and Bathsheba. But we also see this in the plague stories, the famine related to Saul's attempt to break a covenant or David's sin in his census. In every instance, we see that one person's sin damages others and that sin cannot be reduced to something private. To some extent, the fact that we are dealing with sins of the king here makes that more evident than it might be otherwise, precisely because they are such public figures. Yet, even if this reality is less evident in our own experience, it does not take too much reflection to realise that the fallout of our own sin is seldom limited to us alone. This is even more evident in the case of those in Christian leadership, where sin is often profoundly damaging to whole communities.

But even in the midst of what seem like very dark stories here, there is still good news. The remarkable thing is that, even with so much failure and sin, God does not give up. God has made a promise to David, a promise that was a vital step on the way to the gospel of Jesus Christ. And that means that even in the midst of sin and the damage it causes, we see him responding to prayer (and a very brief prayer at that!), taking steps to ensure that his purposes are being worked out. In an imperfect world, God continues to be at work, and his promises continue to be worked out. This is the good news proclaimed here.

FURTHER READING

Bill T. Arnold, *1 and 2 Samuel (The NIV Application Commentary)* (Zondervan, 2003).

David G. Firth, *1 and 2 Samuel: An introduction and survey (Apollos Old Testament Commentary)* (Apollos, 2009).

V. Philips Long, *1 and 2 Samuel: An introduction and commentary (Tyndale Old Testament Commentaries)* (IVP, 2020).

David T. Tsumura, *The Second Book of Samuel (The New International Commentary on the Old Testament)* (Eerdmans, 2019).

Mark 9—11

Steve Motyer

Over this and the next two editions of *Guidelines* we will be reading the second half of Mark's gospel, starting now with three weeks on Mark 9:1—11:10. We will move more slowly through Mark than is usual in *Guidelines*, so the passages for study each day are shorter (six verses on average), enabling us to think in more detail about what we meet.

In this first three-week block we start and end with glory – at the start, with Jesus transfigured on the mountain in front of three amazed disciples (9:2–8), and at the end with him greeted by a great crowd of disciples shouting, 'Hosanna! Blessed is the one who comes in the name of the Lord' as he enters Jerusalem (11:1–10). But 'glory' is not the whole story, as Mark knows so well: this section is marked by two powerful predictions of Jesus' coming suffering and death (9:31 and 10:32–34 – following 8:31), and by some very pointed teaching about discipleship which puts suffering and sacrifice at the heart of following him.

This is Mark's 'travel narrative' (his parallel to Luke 9—19), following Jesus as he travels from Caesarea Philippi, north of Galilee (the probable location of the healing of the epileptic boy in 9:14–27), moves south through Galilee, and then journeys down to Jerusalem via Jericho. 'Following Jesus in the way' – what Bartimaeus does, after receiving his sight (10:52) – is a metaphor for discipleship, and everything that Jesus does and says on this journey contributes to Mark's teaching about what it means to follow him. We are in for a treat.

I have not followed a particular Bible version in writing these notes, because I have usually supplied my own translation when quoting scripture. If not, I indicate the Bible version quoted in brackets.

1 'This is my beloved Son'

Mark 9:1–8

We are at the centre of Mark's gospel here – both literary and theological. This would be obvious, of course, just from the unique nature of this story: the veil draws back, and we glimpse Jesus as he truly is, hidden behind and under all the other stories Mark relates. But the 'voice' of God himself speaking from the cloud, 'This is my beloved Son, hear him!' (v. 7), marks a very particular 'centre' of the gospel.

The last time we heard such a voice was right at the start of the story, at Jesus' baptism, when 'the heavens were rent' (1:10) and the Holy Spirit descended on him accompanied by the voice, 'You are my beloved Son, with you I am pleased!' (1:11). And the gospel will end with a similar group of happenings – Jesus' own 'mighty voice' as he dies, accompanied by the 'rending' (same Greek word) of the temple veil, which symbolised the veil separating heaven and earth, and by the centurion's astonished (and astonishing) confession, 'Truly this man was the Son of God' (15:37–39). Apart from Mark's own introductory confession (1:1), these are the three occasions when Jesus is called 'the Son of God' in the gospel. Two of them bracket the narrative at either end, and 9:7 marks the midpoint, reminding us of the truth which Mark thinks underlies all else.

As God's Son, Jesus represents his Father and speaks from and for him. This status is underlined by the command to 'hear him'. This connects with the appearance of Moses alongside the glorious Jesus, because Moses had told Israel to expect a 'prophet like me' to arise, and he had said, 'You shall *hear* him' – using the same Greek verb, which carries overtones of 'heed' and 'obey' (Deuteronomy 18:15). Here Jesus is identified as the one who fulfils this prophecy, and so from now on we will listen even more carefully to what he says. About this prophet, God says to Moses, 'I will put my words in [his] mouth… Anyone who does not heed the words that the prophet shall speak in my name, I myself will hold accountable' (Deuteronomy 18:18–19, NRSV). We enter the second half of Mark's gospel, therefore, knowing how much is at stake – but also how truly incredible it is that God's glorious Son walks among us, even if Peter (like us, so often) struggles to respond appropriately (v. 5)!

2 Puzzles and prophecies

The command to secrecy (v. 9) is not unusual in Mark (see for example 1:34, 44; 3:12), but it is puzzling. Peter, James and John clearly struggle not only with 'Why?' but also with 'What, precisely?' How long are they to keep secret this revelation of Jesus' glory and true identity? What is this 'resurrection of the Son of Man'?

Jesus' command looks back to his words in 8:31, which Peter failed to grasp then. He still fails. But the puzzle is compounded now by Jesus' further words in 9:1, about the coming of God's kingdom 'with power' within the lifetime of some present. In standard Jewish theology, as taught by 'the scribes' (v. 11), the coming of God's kingdom was an end-time event, linked to the resurrection of Israel and the final judgement of the world. But they also taught – from Malachi 4:5 – that the prophet Elijah would reappear before this 'great and terrible day of the Lord', to make Israel ready. The three disciples have just seen Elijah – was that the prophesied appearance? But it wasn't public, before Israel. And clearly Elijah *can't* make a public appearance, if Jesus' true identity has to be kept secret until the final resurrection.

These are the issues bundled into the disciples' question in verse 11. Jesus' reply (vv. 12–13) in turn needs some teasing out. The background is that John the Baptist was identified by early Christians as this reappearing Elijah – and Matthew makes this explicit in his version of this conversation (Matthew 17:13). 'Elijah indeed comes first to restore all things,' says Jesus (v. 12a): Mark would doubtless like us to remember the huge significance and impact of John's preaching and baptism, summarised in 1:2–8. But (it's important that we imagine a 'but' in the middle of verse 12) that can't be the whole story of the preparation needed before the day of the Lord, because scripture also prophesies the rejection and suffering of 'the Son of Man'. That must take place as well. And we need to remember that the new Elijah's ministry of restoration ended in failure – in imprisonment and execution (Mark 6:14–29). He led many to repentance as prophesied, but he ended up broken on the wheel of intransigent royal pride and cruelty.

Where is this all leading? What is this strange imminent coming 'in power' of God's kingdom? How does it all fit together? We move forward…

3 Power needed

It is often the case that a puzzling Bible saying is deliberately so, and it is meant to stay in our minds as we read further, suggesting questions that might clarify the puzzle in due course. This is certainly the case with Mark 9:1, which leaves us with the question: when will those who heard Jesus see 'the kingdom of God come with power'? The Greek phrasing is interesting – using a perfect participle ('having come'), it implies not an event (the powerful *arrival* of the kingdom) but the realisation of a state of affairs: we see that the kingdom of God has powerfully come.

For those on the lookout, today's story (to be completed tomorrow) begins to suggest an answer. The climax of the story lies not so much in the actual healing of this poor boy – whose dreadful symptoms are described twice, in verses 18 and 22, in addition to the awful manifestation of them in verse 20 – as in the vivid exchange between Jesus and his distracted and desperate father, in verses 22–24. This turns on the issue of power: 'If you can,' says the man – literally: 'If you have the power' – 'pity us and help us!' (v. 22). Jesus immediately picks up this appeal to his own power, and plays it back to the father: 'You say "If you have the power"? All things are within the power of the one who believes' (v. 23). This then elicits one of the most poignant cries in the gospel, as the father bursts out – 'with tears', say some manuscripts – 'I believe! Help my unbelief!' (v. 24).

This 'power' focus is set by the whole scenario as Mark introduces it: Jesus comes down from the mountain into the centre of a vigorous debate caused by the disciples' *failure* to heal this boy (literally, 'they did not have the strength', v. 18). Previously, on their mission, 'they cast out many demons, and anointed with oil many who were sick and healed them' (6:13). But now 'the power' seems to have deserted them. Why? It would be very easy to assume that this is because the power is located in Jesus, and therefore his presence is needed for this healing. But that is *not* Mark's answer. For him – amazingly – the power rests in the shaky and desperate faith of a deeply troubled and loving father who cries out for compassion and 'help'.

4 The power of prayer

The boy's symptoms look very like epilepsy to modern eyes (v. 26; compare v. 18), so it is interesting that Mark, like Jesus, identifies an 'unclean spirit' that needs to be 'thrown out'. The problem here is not an ancient world view that we no longer share, but our modern tendency to separate body from spirit and to regard illnesses as purely physical problems with no possible spiritual aspects or descriptions. In the biblical view, rather, we are 'spirited bodies', to use Nancey Murphy's vivid phrase – bodies which are in themselves spiritual (see her book *Bodies and Souls, or Spirited Bodies?*, Cambridge University Press, 2006). Our *bodies*, not our 'souls', are indwelt by the Holy Spirit; and our *bodies* – without which we do not exist – are the objects of God's redemptive work in Christ. When Paul says that God has 'rescued us from the power of darkness and transferred us to the kingdom of his beloved Son' (Colossians 1:13), he believes that this has happened to our whole selves, including our bodies, and not to some disembodied bit of us. Our bodies are 'limbs of Christ' (1 Corinthians 6:15).

This gives the essential background to stories like this, which vividly illustrate being rescued from the powers of darkness and transferred into God's kingdom. We should not conclude that epilepsy is therefore of the powers of evil – but in the case of this poor boy it definitely was, and Jesus gloriously drives the powers back and raises him up. It is not by chance that Mark uses 'resurrection' language in verse 27, just as he does with Jairus' daughter in 5:41–42: 'Jesus grasped his hand and raised him up – and he rose!' This is kingdom power, released by the faltering faith of the boy's father.

Why couldn't we do that? ask the disciples, away from the crowds. Because you didn't pray, Jesus gently suggests (v. 29). Once again the 'power' word appears: 'This kind [of evil] is expelled by no power except that of prayer.' Prayer is that which brings us into intimacy with our heavenly Father – into the kind of place where Jesus has just been, on the mountain. The kingdom does not come with power through employing the right techniques or using the right words, but simply through prayer that arises from faith – even when (especially when?) the prayer is desperate and the faith is very weak.

5 Trouble ahead

This is the second in a sequence of predictions of Jesus' coming death and resurrection – see also 8:31 and 10:32–34. In all of them Jesus applies the prediction to 'the Son of Man', as though the Son of Man is some other figure and not himself. Why does he do this? This may well be a factor in the disciples' failure to understand what he says (v. 32). We remember Peter, James and John's puzzlement over 'the resurrection of the dead' in 9:10: as good Jews, they knew exactly what 'the resurrection of the dead' was, but it was the connection with 'the Son of Man' (9:9) which was puzzling in that context.

'The Son of Man' is Jesus' favourite self-designation in the gospels. Scholars have long maintained two things about this – first, that Jesus is almost certainly drawing on the vision of 'one like a son of man' in Daniel 7:13–14, where this 'son of man' figure is invested by God with 'dominion, glory and kingdom'; and, second, that the obscurity of this allusion may have meant that people heard it as a rather quaint form of speech, possible in first-century Aramaic, where 'son of man' could be an odd periphrasis for 'I'. Either way, Jesus leaves his hearers – in this case, his disciples – with a puzzle: if they get the allusion to Daniel, why is he associating this glorified figure with suffering and death? And is this himself or someone else? If they don't get it, why is he talking in this odd way? And again, is he referring to himself?

This is an aspect of what used to be called the 'messianic secret' in Mark – the way in which Jesus deliberately veils his identity. We see it here in that 'he did not want anyone to know' that he was back in Galilee (v. 30). In this case Mark gives the reason for the secrecy: verse 31 begins 'For…' But even as Jesus communicates this vital teaching to his disciples, he phrases it in such a way that they fail to understand.

It's not surprising, really. The kingdom of God turns things upside down. It's the weakest, most vulnerable faith that unlocks kingdom power, and the Son of Man rejects human adulation so that he can enter his kingdom through suffering and death. Who would have suspected that?

6 Topsy-turvy kingdom

We dig deeper now into what the disciples are failing to understand about the kingdom of God as it arrives with Jesus (compare 1:15). As they walked 'on the way' with Jesus to Capernaum, they had discussed which of them was 'the greatest'. In other words, they are seeing their association with Jesus as a route to kudos, social advantage, coming out on top: getting glory! Mark uses the phrase 'on the way' twice to give the setting for this discussion (vv. 33–34), and his first readers would have known well that 'the Way' was a shorthand for the *Christian* way, the way of following Christ (see Acts 9:2; 19:9; 24:22). But for Mark this 'way' with Jesus – as he will underline in 10:32 – is the way to Jerusalem, where the Son of Man will 'give his life as a ransom for many' (10:45), scorned and shamed: and his followers must learn that this Way turns their social values upside down. It is not a way to bolster their own status.

Jesus has a pointed message about this just for 'the twelve' (v. 35). They are, after all, the group within the wider company of disciples who might have thought to gain most from following Jesus. Children were valued in ancient society simply as adults-in-preparation. They had no social status of their own. But in God's kingdom it is very different. Jesus places 'a child' – male or female, the silence about gender is significant – at the 'centre' of the group of apostles and identifies himself wholly with him or her: 'Whoever receives one such child in my name receives me,' he says, and then extends that to include God, 'the one who sent me' (v. 37). Behind these words lies the Jewish notion of the *shaliach*, or 'sent one' – the idea that a representative can stand fully for the one who commissioned them. On this basis the twelve have themselves been appointed as 'apostles' ('sent ones', 3:14), and they have already been out on a mission representing Jesus (6:7). But now an insignificant child is promoted into this role! – *standing for* Jesus as a treasure of the kingdom.

This is deeply radical, and Jesus will say more about it in the next chapter (10:13–16), because, as Mark's story develops, it becomes very clear that the twelve found this as hard to comprehend as we do today.

Guidelines

As we look back over our first week of readings in Mark's gospel, it would be good to take a moment to recapture what stands out for you – any features of Mark's story which have particularly touched or spoken to you.

For me, it is the contrast between the two stories with which Mark 9 begins – the transfiguration on the mountain (vv. 2–8) and the healing of the epileptic boy (vv. 14–27). It feels like a classic 'down from the mountaintop' experience! Mark may in fact be alluding to Moses' experience in Exodus 32, when he comes down from the mountain having received the law – his face glowing with God's glory – only to find the Israelites worshipping the golden calf at the bottom. So here, fresh from this amazing encounter with God himself, Jesus and his three disciples are plunged straight into the heart-wrenching experience of the desperate father and his tortured son and into the other disciples' pained inability to help. It seems like the contrast could hardly be sharper, reminding us of times when we too, with an 'Oh no, here we go again!', have had to put aside our own comfort and blessing, to become immersed in the needs and pains of others.

Yes, it's all that, and more: because, for Mark, Jesus does not stop being the glorious Son of God when he comes down the mountain. His glory is merely veiled, just as the name 'Son of God' is veiled under the mysterious 'Son of Man'. The resurrection language used about the boy as he is healed is immediately picked up and applied to Jesus himself; just as the crowd pronounces the boy dead, but then he is raised from death (vv. 26–27), so 'the Son of Man will be betrayed into the hands of men, and they will kill him, but three days after death he will rise!' (v. 31). The glory of this Son of God is expressed through his identification with the poorest and the most afflicted – he shares their fate, just as he then identifies himself with 'a little child' (v. 36). This is truly good news (1:1)!

1 'In the name of Jesus'

Mark 9:38–41

This passage and tomorrow's develop a discussion about Jesus' mind-blowing statement, that he is represented in and by a small child (9:37). If that is true, what are the implications for the status of those who have committed themselves to being his proper, signed-up disciples? In fact this question, with related issues, takes us right through to the end of chapter 10.

John – one of the inner circle, the extra-special one within the twelve (9:2) – raises the issue of someone using Jesus' name as a talisman in exorcisms. Using powerful names (usually of gods) was a regular feature in magic and other supernatural practices, including exorcism: the power of the name was invoked to give power to the ritual. 'We tried to stop him,' says John, 'because he wasn't following us!' (v. 38). Jesus' reply again picks up the 'power' language which, as we saw last week, ultimately looks back to that mysterious saying about the coming of the kingdom in power with which this whole section of Mark begins (9:1). 'Don't hinder him,' Jesus says, 'for no one who exercises "power" in my name will find that he has the power, soon after, to denigrate me. For whoever is not against us is really on our side' (vv. 39–40). In fact, he adds, anyone who gives them the smallest gift 'because you bear Christ's name' will not miss out on a reward (v. 41).

John – and his fellow disciples – lived in a world in which loyalty to your group (your teacher, your tribe, your family, your people) was everything. These loyalties defined identity, and they created distinctions and rivalries. So how can the disciples gain a sense of what it means to follow Jesus as 'Messiah' (compare 8:29) if the 'power' of his name can be deployed by any Tom, Dick or Harry? Does he not have a proper school, proper boundaries around belonging, proper exclusion of non-members?

Yes, you can 'belong' to the Christ, as Jesus implies in verse 41 – the gifts are given to a distinct group. But this is definitely a group with permeable boundaries and a wonderful openness to the power of God's kingdom showing up anywhere. The church has always struggled with this – and we still do. It would be so much easier to be the sole place of God's power at work in the world. If only! God, it appears, is much more untidy than that – much more profligate with his grace.

2 Take care

Jesus continues his reply to John (v. 38) with some very sobering warnings and challenges. It's not just a matter of allowing people outside the signed-up group to exercise kingdom power; the disciples also need to watch out, in case they lose the privilege of belonging. Specifically, if they cause 'one of these little ones who believe in me' to trip up (v. 42), it would be better for them to suffer the most awful imaginable end… (*unspoken thought*: … than to fall into the hands of God the judge). Implicit here is the amazing claim that God's judgement will be severe indeed against anyone who causes harm to a 'little one' who believes in Jesus.

In Matthew's version of this saying it is clear that the 'little ones' in mind are children, like the child here in verse 36 (see Matthew 18:5–6). Mark may intend the same, or maybe for him these 'little ones who believe' include any who look to the twelve for guidance and end up stumbling. So much is at stake! In fact, the disciples need to take great care that *they themselves* don't end up stumbling. The sayings in verses 43–48 could hardly be more vivid, and they may reflect real practices in some cultures surrounding Israel, where the amputation of hands or feet was a prescribed punishment for various crimes – sometimes as a substitute for the death penalty. Jesus is speaking metaphorically, however, encouraging a very careful self-discipline so that ultimately his disciples may 'enter the kingdom of God' (v. 47) and not be thrown into Gehenna (Jerusalem's ever-burning rubbish-tip, which came to symbolise the future destruction of the wicked).

There is no automatic guarantee that those who are 'in' – even in the inner three, like John – will ultimately enter the kingdom coming soon with power (9:1). How can they make sure they don't stumble? Verses 49–50 give the answer, in an amazing mixture of metaphors: God's 'fire' will purify them so that they can be truly 'salty', full of savour. They had probably seen little piles of useless rock salt out of which the rain had gradually leached all the salt. Maybe the last phrase unpacks these metaphors, looking back undoubtedly to their dispute about greatness in verse 34: 'Live at peace with one another!' (v. 50b). That's the key. 'Peace' means accepting each other, not treating each other as rivals.

3 Live at peace... and divorce?

The command to 'live at peace with one another' (9:50) leads in a surprising direction, as Mark now records an encounter with some Pharisees who want to 'test' Jesus on the issue of divorce (v. 2). This was a hot topic between rival Pharisaic schools: the disciples of Rabbi Shammai took a hard line, maintaining that divorce should only be for adultery, while the disciples of Rabbi Hillel interpreted Moses' permission (Deuteronomy 24:1–4, cited here in verse 4) much less strictly. With whom will Jesus side?

The answer is, with neither. Neither Pharisaic school referred to Genesis 1:27 and 2:24 when debating divorce, as Jesus does here (vv. 6–8). He takes the question back to first principles and teaches that marriage is about 'two becoming one' before God. 'That which God has joined, let not humans divide' is his conclusion (v. 9) – in other words, divorce is in principle a violation of the institution of marriage, and therefore should not happen.

The disciples are horrified. In Matthew they react, 'If this is how the matter stands between a man and his wife, it is better not to marry!' (Matthew 19:10). In interpreting Jesus' teaching, we need to remember two things. First, he is reacting to the Pharisaic debate which he thinks starts in the wrong place and therefore lands up with lax and abusive marital practices, with wives being dismissed for trivial reasons – at least in the case of the Hillelites. Second, it would be wrong to hear him implying that Moses should never have given the divorce permission. Yes, divorce always means violating the commandments (vv. 11–12) and breaking something precious to God, but sometimes it is the only way to 'live at peace with one another,' because *hearts are still hard*. The reason motivating Moses' permission (v. 5) still applies.

Jesus' basic position with the law is that it stands (see Matthew 5:17–19), even if – as here – he sharpens up and reshapes its contemporary interpretation and application. He does not disallow Moses. So to hear Jesus' teaching as an absolute prohibition of divorce under all circumstances is not only wrong, but in principle opens the door to abuse of a different kind – condemning people to stay in a relationship they ought to flee. There are never any easy answers! But the command to 'live at peace' is Jesus' basic summons here.

We will come back to this thorny issue in *Guidelines* at the end of the week.

4 Back to the child

It is really interesting that these words on children follow, because then – as now – small children are always the ones who suffer most when their parents divorce, and their feelings can easily be overlooked. And how shocking these words are! There are two shocking things here. First, Mark tells us that Jesus was 'annoyed' (v. 14) – not an emotion we readily associate with him. And second, verse 15 – introduced with a solemn 'Truly, I tell you' – makes an almost incredible statement about entry into the kingdom of God. If Jesus hadn't said it, we would never have made it up.

The translations tend to sanctify the feeling. 'Jesus was indignant' is a favourite (NRSV, NIV, ESV, NEB, etc.), because indignation focuses on the action, whereas annoyance focuses on the actors, the people responsible for the action. And this is definitely the latter, as it will be in 10:41, when the rest of the twelve will be 'annoyed' at James and John (the same word). Jesus is *annoyed* that the twelve are just not getting it: did they not see him embracing a child in their midst just a few verses ago (9:36)? Did they not even begin to understand what he said about that child (9:37)? How can they actually *stop* children coming to him now? One of the great (and encouraging) features of Mark is that he is so open about the disciples' frailties, and in particular that they were so slow on the uptake. If they were, we are allowed to be, too!

Maybe Jesus' annoyance feeds into the amazing thing he says in verses 14b–15, as he embraces the children who come to him. The negative is extra-emphatic – 'Truly I tell you, whoever does not receive the kingdom of God as a little child will never, ever enter it!' This goes beyond what he says in 9:37 about the child representing him. Even more, the child must represent *us* – must represent to us that ideal human being acceptable to God and welcomed into his kingdom. What is it about the child that holds that ideal? Is it innocence, trustingness, playfulness, simplicity? We can speculate, but actually Mark is going to let us know in the passages that follow (and it's none of these).

It would be appropriate today to pray for God's blessing on children known to you – bring them to Jesus like the parents in verse 13.

5 Back to basics

Verse 21a is deeply moving and encouraging: 'Jesus, looking into him, loved him, and said…' Here 'look' is a compound verb with the connotation that Jesus could see beyond the surface to his heart, and he *loves* this young man despite all the complexity and dividedness of his motivation. This is the counterpart to Jesus' annoyance in verse 14! He loves us even when we are torn in our devotion to him.

What does he see in this man? His eagerness and intense spiritual longing, for sure – signalled in Mark's vivid description of him 'running' up to Jesus and 'kneeling' before him. He wants to be sure that he will 'inherit eternal life' (v. 17), that is, that he will indeed enter the kingdom of God. Deflecting him from his own authority (v. 18), Jesus points him to the commandments (v. 19). Scripture has a full and sufficient answer to his question. 'But Teacher,' he says, 'all these I have kept from my youth' (v. 20). That last phrase, 'from my youth', is the key to this passage. What has happened to this young man since his 'youth' – since he was like the children whom Jesus was embracing and blessing in verse 16?

Answer: he grew up and inherited his wealth. We don't know that yet; Mark saves that up for the last line of the story (v. 22). But Jesus sees it all, and sees clearly what this man needs to do if he is to 'receive the kingdom of God like a little child' (v. 15). He needs to give all that money up – in fact, to go back to the position of unquestioning dependence and powerlessness which marked his life as a child. 'One thing you lack: go, sell what you have and give it to the poor, and you will have treasure in heaven – and then come and follow me!' (v. 21b).

That's what children are like – not cute, playful, innocent or pure, but *powerless* and without status and desire for it; and, of course, without the money that can confer status, respect and security. That's how we need to be, in order to enter the kingdom of God.

Jesus is talking about our hearts. We could give away our houses and bank accounts and still long for the status, power and security that come from having our own stuff piled around us. Give up that longing, he says. Follow me!

6 'The love of money is the root of all evil'

We should probably imagine Jesus indoors again with his disciples, reflecting on what has just happened (compare 9:33; 10:10). And once again Jesus delivers a statement which staggers his disciples (v. 24) – 'How tough it is for those with money to enter the kingdom of God!' (v. 23). Famously he then expands this with a picture which was surely meant to have them chuckling as well as underlining the serious point – 'It's easier to get a camel through the eye of a needle than a rich man into the kingdom of God!' (v. 25). This is particularly staggering for his disciples, because they will have assumed – as their culture generally did – that riches are a sign of God's blessing. Hence their amazement in verse 26, where 'completely bowled over' would be an appropriate translation – 'Who then can be saved?'

We could expand their comment like this: the wealthy, the powerful and the aristocrats are the obvious candidates for salvation, because they are the ones whom God has obviously blessed already with his favour. So if they're not saved, who can be? Although the Old Testament envisages the possibility of being wicked and wealthy (e.g. Psalm 73:3–12) – and indeed of being righteous and poor (remember Job) – the close connection between obedience and prosperity in important passages like Deuteronomy 28 meant that people naturally argued the other way round: if you were prospering, then you must be righteous (and if you are poor, then almost certainly you are not).

Jesus recalibrates the whole arrangement in verse 27, once again using the 'power' language which keeps cropping up in connection with the kingdom of God: 'Seeing them deeply [Mark uses the same word as in verse 21], Jesus said, "Salvation is beyond human power, but not beyond God's. For everything is within God's power."' Salvation is not a matter of merit and reward, but simply (and wholly) of God's grace powerfully acting beyond our capacity, to bring us back to childhood before him (v. 15). John's version of this saying appears in the famous dialogue between Jesus and the wealthy aristocrat Nicodemus: 'Truly truly I tell you, unless you are born from above, you cannot see the kingdom of God' (John 3:3). When the kingdom comes with power, it touches people irrespective of age, rank, wealth, learning, gender and (of course) race.

Guidelines

Mark 10:2–12 (with its parallel in Matthew 19:3–9) is the key passage on divorce in Jesus' teaching. In the note above I took a particular line on its interpretation, suggesting that Mark 10:9 ('That which God has joined, let not humans divide') should not be understood in an absolutist way to mean that every marriage is indissoluble and continues to exist in God's eyes, even if the couple have long since separated or been divorced in a human court. I tried to give good reasons for this view, but it's not the view that churches have generally taken of marriage.

There are plenty of books on this, and if *Guideliness* readers want to follow this up, I'd recommend (following the traditional interpretation) William Heth and Gordon Wenham, *Jesus and Divorce* (Hodder and Stoughton, 1984) or Andrew Cornes, *Divorce and Remarriage: Biblical principles and pastoral practice* (Christian Focus Publications, 2002); and giving a different viewpoint, like the one I follow here, David Instone-Brewer, *Divorce and Remarriage in the Church: Biblical solutions for pastoral realities* (Paternoster, 2003) or – more scholarly – David Instone-Brewer, *Divorce and Remarriage in the Bible: The social and literary context* (Eerdmans, 2002).

As we've seen this week, the great burden of Jesus' teaching in this section of Mark is the surprising way in which God's kingdom upsets human expectations of rank, status, order and value. The divorce teaching fits into this because – I believe – Jesus is seeking to 'level up' a situation in which women were easily exploited and treated with injustice by men who interpreted the 'something objectionable' in Deuteronomy 24:1 (NRSV) to suit themselves. In 10:12, while underlining that divorce is not God's will, Jesus actually envisages that women can divorce their husbands – virtually unknown in the first century (though Herodias did it; see Mark 6:17), but allowed in Exodus 21:10–11.

1 Giving up everything

Mark 10:28–31

It seems like Peter – one of the inner three, who went up the mountain with Jesus (9:2) – may be getting the point. He's grasped that following Jesus is not about gaining, but about giving up: 'Look – we have left everything and followed you' (v. 28). Here, the verbs are the same as those used to describe Peter's response to Jesus in 1:18, matched immediately afterwards by James and John abandoning their nets, their boat and their father (1:19–20).

But once again Jesus wants to qualify his understanding. 'Giving up' is not the whole story. With another powerful 'Truly I tell you' saying, Jesus first lists seven things which people might give up 'for my sake, and for the sake of the gospel' (v. 29) – all of them likely to be true for the twelve, in different measures. But then he re-lists six of the seven as also *gains* for his disciples, 'one hundredfold, now in the present time', before adding soberingly 'with persecutions – and in the age to come, eternal life' (v. 30).

Jesus has already claimed a replacement family for himself, in 3:31–35: when his mother and brothers arrived, he pointedly did not respond to their summons, and 'looking round at those sitting in a circle around him said, "Here are my mother and my brothers! For whoever does the will of God, that person is my brother and sister and mother."' Doubtless this is what he has in mind in today's passage – the fellowship of his disciples provides a replacement family worth far more, even if it comes 'with persecutions'. This probably explains why 'father' is omitted from the second list: his disciples have one new Father, in heaven (compare Matthew 23:9).

What about the presence of 'fields' in the second list, repeated from the first? There is more here than meets the eye, for in theory each family in Israel lived on a parcel of land given to them by God. There had been much disturbance since the original settlement in Joshua, but the feeling of attachment to their land as a divine gift was shared in Israel. It went with attachment to family. To sacrifice this 'for my sake, and for the sake of the gospel' was a huge step to take, a step which implicitly called into question Israel's whole covenant relation with God.

But Jesus claims that his followers get 'fields' back. What can he mean? The story of Bartimaeus will help us here, which we will look at shortly.

2 Horrors coming

We have noticed before how 'the way' has a symbolic flavour (see 9:33–34) – not just the physical path, but also the path of discipleship. So here: 'They were on the way, going up to Jerusalem' (v. 32). This is the path of discipleship which Jesus must tread, and his disciples are following him, but with astonishment and with fear. There is something about Jesus' determined step which really frightens them. So we read that he 'takes the twelve aside again' and gives the third and most detailed prediction of his passion (compare 8:31; 9:31). We must imagine him extracting the twelve from the general crowd of disciples, taking them off to the side of the road and delivering this bombshell. This is too huge a revelation for the disciples as a whole – they can't cope with it.

It must have been almost too much for the twelve. On both previous occasions, Mark tells us that they did not understand what he was saying – 'and were afraid to ask' (9:32). On this occasion, Mark doesn't comment about their reaction, but Jesus' language is so vivid, so detailed and so unmistakable, that maybe we should imagine a stunned, horrified silence. They are beginning to get the message, and they are appalled and afraid. How will they react? We shall see.

Jesus describes this coming torture once again as the experience of 'the Son of Man'. It is not just *as himself* that he will be condemned, tortured and killed, but as the Son of Man, that is, in his Danielic identity as the 'one like a son of man' who is given kingdom and royal power by 'the Ancient of Days' (Daniel 7:13–14). The paradox claimed here, both by Jesus and by Mark, is simply huge – that God gives his kingdom and his power to one who is rejected, condemned, tortured and killed by the human 'powers' of the day, both Jewish (v. 33) and Gentile (v. 34), before he rises to the glory Daniel saw.

As we will see shortly, this is the absolute basis of the turning-upside-down of the human power and status pyramid throughout this section of Mark – a pyramid which of course normally had God at the top, ensuring the proper position of all the layers of social privilege and non-privilege below. How different is God's kingdom? As we read yesterday, 'Many who are first shall be last – and the last first!' (10:31).

3 Well, at least they're upfront about it!

Mark 10:35–40

In verse 28 we heard from one of the three 'top' disciples who went up the mountain with Jesus – now we hear from the other two, James and John. In Matthew's version of this conversation it's initiated by their mum, who wants the top spot for her sons (Matthew 20:20–23). But even in Matthew, Jesus' reply is to the sons themselves, not to her. Here in Mark they take responsibility for the whole approach, even beginning it with that ploy so familiar to parents the world over, 'Promise you'll do whatever I ask?'

But at least that approach shows how familiar and comfortable they are with Jesus. We can imagine a shy grin on their faces as they sidle up to him with their request. But what a misunderstanding! Mark is so open about how *hard* it is truly to grasp the radical re-ordering of social relationships involved in the kingdom of God. James and John have indeed got the message that Jesus is going to die soon, and they believe that he is the Messiah, the Son of God – so as two of the top three they think it's not too much to ask that they should sit on either side of Jesus in his 'glory'. Their reference to his 'glory' looks back to his words in 8:38 – they have indeed been listening.

Jesus' response, 'You don't know what you are asking for,' means, 'You don't know what it would mean, to be given one of those exalted places.' It would mean that they had trodden the same 'way' of suffering that he is following. Are they ready to share his 'baptism', his 'cup' (v. 38)? Rather than shoving their noses in the suffering that would await them, Jesus uses these two allusive metaphors. Yes, of course we are, they say, leaving the meaning unclear. Well, you shall, says Jesus, but it's not mine to say who will end up beside me in glory. It's 'for those for whom it has been prepared' (v. 40) – which may, of course, be James and John. They can still hope.

Jesus treats them with such love and respect, but they are still locked into the old way of thinking about status, which puts them in competition with their fellow disciples. Tomorrow we hear more from Jesus on this.

4 The bottom line

We've been moving towards these verses ever since the power of the kingdom was revealed through the desperate and trembling faith of a tortured father (9:22–25). They represent a mini-climax to this teaching section of Mark in which the *shape of discipleship* has been a prominent focus. Annoyed by James and John – inevitably the word got out – the other ten apostles find themselves immediately summoned to a pow-wow. Mark suggests that Jesus addresses just 'the ten', but he doesn't exclude the thought that James and John, maybe somewhat red-faced, are also there to hear these amazing words – four verses of groundbreaking teaching about Christian leadership and community which the church has struggled ever since to realise in practice, even when we have managed to grasp it in theory.

The exercise of power in God's kingdom is completely different from worldly norms. 'It is not so among you,' says Jesus, commenting on the standard pattern of social hierarchy and power among 'the Gentiles'. It is interesting that he does not say 'it *must not* be so among you': he is not giving an aspiration, but describing a state of affairs. In the kingdom it *is* simply the case that 'whoever wants to be great among you will be your servant, and whoever wants to be first among you will be the slave of all' (vv. 43–44). No one without that qualification (servant, slave) will ever be 'great' or 'first' in the kingdom. And 'slave' is a powerful word: these are the lowest of the low in Greco-Roman society, with no rights, privileges or powers. Paul loved to call himself 'slave of Christ Jesus' (Romans 1:1; 1 Corinthians 7:22; Galatians 1:10, etc.), and added, 'We announce ourselves as your slaves too, for Jesus' sake' (2 Corinthians 4:5).

Paul certainly 'got' this message, in his exercise of power and leadership, and he 'got', too, that it is because of Jesus and the cross that things are shaped this way in his church. This is what Jesus himself says here, in the famous verse 45, which begins with an unexpressed thought – 'And, *however surprising it may be, this is the right style for leadership among you*, for the Son of Man did not come to be served, but to serve, and to give his life as a ransom for many.' It all starts with that steady tread of Jesus on the way to Jerusalem.

5 Blind Bartimaeus

Fittingly, this section of the gospel ends with Jesus' last healing miracle in Mark, which pulls together and illustrates many of the themes in the preceding narrative. Here we have a blind man who already has remarkable (in)sight. He can see clearly who Jesus is – the Son of David, the Messiah – and knows what he must do. He's a man with absolutely nothing, who has already lost his 'place', his land and presumably also his family, for they are not caring for him. And he abandons what little he has to come to Jesus, chiefly his cloak, which beggars would normally spread on the ground in front of them to collect gifts (v. 50).

When he cries out in faith, Jesus stops. The crowd tells this disreputable nobody to be quiet (v. 48), but he somehow knows that Jesus will listen, and he doubles the volume. His cry is for 'mercy', from a place of open, unconcealed need. He has no status, money or achievement with which to earn Jesus' attention and healing. But that's what opens the door! He rests on nothing but Jesus' mercy towards people like him and his merciful power to heal, and no embarrassment or disapproval or public shame will stop him from asserting his case and standing before Jesus with his heartfelt request. When Bartimaeus speaks to Jesus, he calls him 'Rabbouni' (v. 51) – *my* rabbi – a term of greater intimacy and connection than just 'Rabbi', used by Peter on the mountain in 9:5. (Elsewhere in the gospels, 'Rabbouni' only appears on the lips of Mary when she meets the risen Jesus in the garden of Gethsemane in John 20:16.)

And then Bartimaeus joins Jesus 'in the way' (v. 52, the last words of the story), finding place and home in the company of his disciples (compare v. 30). He has been 'ransomed' by the Son of Man (v. 45), one of the 'many' for whom the Son of Man dies. And when we see that the 'many' doesn't just reluctantly include figures like Bartimaeus at the end of the queue, but that he is actually *typical* of the target population – he, first and foremost, smelly, loud, homeless and uneducated but full of faith – then we begin to get a clear sense of what God's kingdom, ushered in by this Son of Man, is going to look like.

6 Into Jerusalem

Mark 11:1–10

Today's story is a kind of bridge passage – both ending the section of Mark we've read in these three weeks and beginning the next. The question is, after all the extraordinary teaching we've had about the upside-down nature of the kingdom of God under the rule of 'the Son of Man', how will he arrive in Jerusalem, the centre of God's earthly kingdom? How will this 'son of David' (10:47) arrive in the city of David's throne? It's interesting that we tradition-ally call this 'the triumphal entry', because instinctively we feel that it must be massive. It must be an entry fit for a King, capital 'K'! And this is certainly the direction in which Matthew takes this story, underlining the fulfilment of Zechariah's messianic prophecy in Jesus' action (Matthew 21:4–5) and adding 'when Jesus entered Jerusalem, the whole city was shaken with the question "Who is this?"' (Matthew 21:10).

But this is not how Mark tells it. There is no hint here that the crowd hail-ing Jesus is other than the group of disciples who have travelled with him. Matthew helps us by explaining Jesus' strange action in acquiring the colt on which he rides the last stage – Jesus is deliberately creating a 'sign' for those who have eyes to see. But Mark leaves it unexplained, and even leaves ambiguity (especially developed by Luke, in fact) around the words the two disciples are given to say about the colt (v. 3): 'the Lord has need of it' can mean 'his owner needs it', as though they are simply on an errand from the donkey's real owner. But of course they are! This Son of Man has all power and kingdom, including ownership of all donkeys… except that his power and kingdom *appears* so differently.

Taking their hint from Jesus, his disciples do their best to put on a show, adopting festal language and actions from the festival of Tabernacles (vv. 8–10), although there is no indication that it is that time of year (and we gather later that in fact Jesus arrives in Jerusalem not long before Pass-over). They want people to know who they think he is (v. 10)! But there is no indication that their words, or the event, created any headlines. Hardly 'triumphal'. The king arrives pretty much incognito – although 'Hosanna in the highest' is an appropriate cry for those who have the eyes to see.

Guidelines

Again, it would be good to reflect on what has struck you most this week: what in particular do you take with you from these readings?

Mark 10:31 and 45 sit at the heart of the theology of the kingdom developed here, offering us a view of power which completely subverts 'normal' views of leadership and social hierarchy. It is interesting that this view of servant leadership has gained some traction in recent secular writing about the best way to lead. Leadership which is not 'top down', but which aims above all to empower the talents, ideas and contribution of all in an organisation, is much more effective in the long run.

This should be supremely true in the church. Paul works this out using his metaphor of the church as a body – 'the body of Christ,' he says (see especially 1 Corinthians 12:12–31). Every member of the body has a unique gift to exercise, a ministry distributed by the Holy Spirit. So while it is still true to say that the church has '*first*, apostles' (1 Corinthians 12:28), this does not mean that the apostles of the church receive the first honour, before all the rest of us. It means that their teaching is the foundation (Ephesians 2:20), at the bottom, not at the top.

C.S. Lewis expresses this beautifully in his imaginary bus-tour around heaven and hell in *The Great Divorce* (Geoffrey Bles, 1946). A beautiful and glowing angelic creature appears at the centre of a joyful procession – 'A person of particular importance?' asks the narrator. Oh yes, the tour guide replies, 'She is one of the great ones… Her name on earth was Sarah Smith and she lived at Golders Green!' She was an unknown 'housewife' on earth who simply lived out of the love of God with all she met. Greatness is measured entirely differently in his kingdom.

FURTHER READING

James R. Edwards, *The Gospel According to Mark (The Pillar New Testament Commentary)* (Eerdmans/Apollos, 2002).

Morna D. Hooker, *The Gospel According to St Mark (Black's New Testament Commentaries)* (Continuum, 1991).

William L. Lane, *The Gospel of Mark (The New International Commentary on the New Testament)* (Eerdmans, 1995).

Tom Wright, *Mark for Everyone* (SPCK, 2001).

For books on the issue of divorce raised in this section of Mark, see suggestions in the 'Guidelines' section at the end of the second week.

Developing and practising spiritual disciplines for today

Sally Nash

As I was discipled into faith as a teenager, spiritual disciplines were presented largely as an individualistic activity, initially focusing on the 'quiet time': prayer and Bible study at the beginning of each day. While I have largely kept this discipline, I have added others along the way as my understanding has broadened.

I am now much clearer that spiritual disciplines are something that we can do together as well as alone and that we learn so much from each other as well as God. Our Common Ground Community meets twice a month: once for a meal and a Bible study, usually studying a gospel chapter by chapter, and again over a bring-and-share Sunday lunch when we explore different aspects of our rule and dimensions of our life and discipleship. Dietrich Bonhoeffer's book *Life Together* is a good example of some of the issues we face as we engage in spiritual disciplines together.

I did some crowdsourcing on social media for these notes, and I am grateful to those who helped me refine my thinking around which spiritual disciplines are particularly apt for today. For many of us, online engagement has become an integral part of how we practise our spiritual disciplines, for example praying for our friends or followers, although such connectivity is perhaps also a significant distraction at times. I have appreciated, too, reading and engaging with a variety of spiritual traditions as I have reflected on the spiritual disciplines I have written about, and I am aware that there is treasure and wisdom to be found in so many places.

'Doing what brings me life' is my key thought when thinking about spiritual disciplines: doing what helps me feel more connected to God and God's world, myself and others.

Unless otherwise stated, Bible quotations are taken from the NRSV.

1 Developing a rule and rhythm – purposeful habits

John 15:1–17

The metaphors of abiding in the vine and of God as the vine grower or gardener are ones that have sustained me for many years. While I am not a great gardener, I have tried to develop a rule and rhythm that helps me to be fruitful, which is why I have chosen this passage to reflect on for this spiritual discipline: 'I… appointed you so that you might go and bear fruit – fruit that will last' (v. 16). Flourishing in ministry requires me to be rooted, pruned and nurtured; my rule and rhythm does that. The gardener is purposeful in their habits to enable the fruit to flourish; developing my rule and rhythm with God and his word means I have a purposeful way of living.

As I regularly review my rule and rhythm, I reflect on what needs pruning from it (v. 2). I am in danger sometimes of saying 'yes' to things I should say 'no' to, just because I can do them and I want to be helpful. As seasons in my life and circumstances change, my rhythm needs to change, and as the Holy Spirit moves in different aspects of my life and ministry, adjustment may be necessary (v. 5). It is very easy to get stuck in a rut and lose the joy in things which should be life-giving, and I want God's joy in me (v. 11). I need to regularly pray about what I am doing and where my energy should be focused. Now, there are some things which are clear and not negotiable: time with God, worshipping with God's people, time with close family, a proper day of rest – those are integral to obeying God's commandments.

We have a corporate rule as part of the Common Ground Community which reflects verses 11–15. Together as disciples of Jesus (in John 15, Jesus is addressing his disciples), we seek to be fruitful, to love one another and to obey God's commandments in the way that seems right for us, in this time and in this place. Each year, we reflect on the seven elements of our common rule and seek to be accountable in how we live it out. Personally, I use the image of the marker posts and shelters that line the pilgrim's way to Holy Island to frame my rhythm of life, and I find that they provide some boundaries to what I do.

2 Simplicity – seeing what matters most in a complex world

Matthew 6:19–34

Many years ago, when I was transitioning from my chosen career to being employed in Christian ministry (raising personal support), I embroidered a small plaque which said, 'Consider the lilies' (v. 28). I still have it. This verse and the promises inherent in the passage continue to sustain me, as I am sometimes naturally cautious and understand the temptation of the words of the serpent to Eve, 'Did God say…?' (Genesis 3:1). There are echoes also of Deuteronomy 28:1–14, which talks about blessings for obedience. Having one response to what matters most – seeking God's kingdom – helps with embracing simplicity as a spiritual discipline.

Jesus was addressing these words to his disciples, so I think it is reasonable to assume that he was speaking into their situation, that they were concerned about what he mentions in verses 25–31: food, drink, clothing. I wonder how those who are in absolute poverty might read these words. However, I think that Jesus would address that situation differently, as the Bible echoes with injunctions for us to care for the poor (e.g. Deuteronomy 10:18). This thought encourages me towards simplicity; as it is often said, 'Live simply that others may simply live.' The first section of the passage for today reminds us not to 'store up for yourselves treasures on earth… but store up for yourselves treasures in heaven' (vv. 19–20). This is often through the way we act towards others, the way we follow God's command to love our neighbour as ourselves.

Simplicity in life is both an aim and a practice. In a society where consumerism is both rampant and contested, making lifestyle choices that have a positive impact on the planet is being seen as increasingly vital. Graham Cray, who was team leader of Fresh Expressions in the Church of England, has done significant thinking about the missional impact of our spiritual practices. In a conversation with me, he suggested that simplicity is related to contentment and helps us to make choices in the light of what matters most, in what for many of us is a complicated and confusing world.

3 Encountering God through creation

We arrived in the village at night. We looked up and, as our eyes adjusted to the darkness, we could see more stars than we had ever seen before. The longer we looked, the more we saw. I was overcome with awe at the immenseness of our creator God and, just as the psalmist was, aware of the smallness of me (v. 4). I experienced with the psalmist that 'the heavens are telling the glory of God' (19:1). Encountering God sometimes feels easier in the midst of his creation. When we read through the gospels, we see how Jesus regularly used nature to teach (Luke 8:4–15) and spent time alone with God away from others (Luke 5:16). Indeed, Colossians 1:15–20 tells us that he redeemed all of creation through the cross.

Psalm 8 begins and ends with the statement, 'O Lord, our Sovereign, how majestic is your name in all the earth!' God can be experienced anywhere. I once did a small research project with a group of students and asked them where they find it easiest to pray. Their answer was in creation, outside. This experience has been repeated many times over as I talk to people about where they feel close to God. Research shows that walking outside benefits physical and mental health, and spiritual disciplines which engage with whole-person well-being are good to practise corporately. So an awareness walk outside, where we look for signs of God, benefits us in so many ways. Forest Church (see Williams, 2019) is a contemporary expression of a corporate encounter with God outdoors, and Muddy Church is an intergenerational outside activity. As we spend time in nature, biblical images can come more alive for us. I always experience hope when I see a rainbow in the sky, not least because of the way that God has spoken to me through them at some very difficult periods of my life.

Our connectedness to and responsibility for creation are integral to Psalm 8: 'You have given them dominion over the works of your hands' (v. 6). Many of us are trying to take that responsibility seriously through making choices which are good for the earth and which address climate change challenges – and we can see that as a spiritual practice.

4 Random acts of kindness – taking God's love into the world

Colossians 3:1–17

Random acts of kindness remind me of God's grace: they are undeserved and, as recipients of them, we are often grateful and give glory to God. The author of Colossians (scholars dispute whether it was Paul) encourages us to live the new life as Christians. Part of this is to clothe ourselves with 'compassion, kindness, humility, meekness, and patience' (v. 12). These are virtues that as Christians we should manifest. There is a meme doing the rounds on social media regularly: 'If you can be anything, be kind.' What does that mean?

Collins English Dictionary defines kindness as 'the quality of being gentle, caring and helpful' and a kindness as 'a helpful, considerate act'. These Bible reading notes have been improved by the kindness of those who took time to comment on my Facebook post, some of them people I do not know in real life. I still remember, over 30 years later, the profound kindness of a very pregnant friend who would not let me drive the 60 miles back home the morning I heard my Dad had unexpectedly died, and that of another friend who came that far to help with the catering at the wake.

Think back over the past week, particularly if you have been out and about. Reflect on how you felt when (if) people treated you kindly and vice versa. Kindness is one of the fruit of the Spirit (Galatians 5:22), and 1 Corinthians 13:1–3 tells us that without love what we do may count as nothing. It is, of course, easy to be kind to those who are kind to us, but we will meet many, sadly, who demonstrate 'anger, wrath, malice, slander, and abusive language' (v. 8). Being kind in such circumstances can be much harder, and we may need to ask God daily to clothe us with compassion and kindness.

In the past, our church has participated in the 'Love life, live Lent' programme. This encourages random acts of kindness, and I have been encouraged by our weekly time of testimony, telling stories of what God did through our actions. I am reminded of the words of Jesus: 'Just as you did it to one of the least of these… you did it to me' (Matthew 25:40). Radical hospitality can also be an outworking of this. Whom do we invite or include and in what ways do we intentionally engage with 'the stranger'? One of the rooms in our church Community House has been used to house asylum seekers, both short and long term, as part of our corporate hospitality.

5 Gazing on the face of Christ – understanding our belovedness

Psalm 27

When Moses came down from the mountain after meeting with God, his face was radiant (Exodus 34:29). The psalmist reflects a desire for this. '"Come," my heart says, "seek his face!" Your face, Lord, do I seek' (v. 8). This is a spiritual discipline I have come to interpret later in life as looking literally at an image of Jesus, as opposed to a metaphorical interpretation. My favourite image of Jesus to gaze upon is the stained-glass window in the Chapel of the Blessed Sacrament at Buckfast Abbey in Devon. I encounter the love of Jesus in a way that is hard to explain, but it enhances my understanding that I am beloved of Christ. That is healing and transformative.

I have chosen to write about this spiritual discipline in part because of my academic study on shame. Several authors talk about the importance of this practice to help people experience a sense of love and acceptance from God. When we feel shame, we tend to turn our face away or look to cover our face. But God does not want us to hide from him. This is why he asks Adam and Eve, 'Where are you?' (Genesis 3:9). As we gaze on Christ's face with love, he wants to reciprocate that gaze, and that helps in our restoration.

In an increasingly visual culture, using pictures rather than words is sometimes more helpful. 'To behold the beauty of the Lord' (v. 4) can be done in many ways, but I commend trying it with a representation of Jesus that resonates with you. From my childhood onwards, there have been images of Jesus I have carried with me, which enable me to say, 'The Lord is my light and salvation; whom shall I fear?' (v. 1). But it is only more recently that I have discovered that stilling myself in front of an image of Christ helps me fully embrace the truth of those words.

6 Living life distinctively

The idea of living life distinctively may not obviously connect to spiritual disciplines, but it enables us to think about the questions 'What does it mean to follow God today?' and 'What difference to my life does my faith make?' Isaiah 58 is part of what is commonly called Second Isaiah (chapters 40—55) and is written to those who have returned to Jerusalem after their exile in Babylon. The Israelites seem to be going through some of the motions of their practices from the past, but to no good effect. In fact, they are living lives that are in contrast to God's hopes and expectations for his people. Their relationships with their neighbours, each other and their God were not right.

Verses 6 and 7 talk about what faithful living looked like in relation to neighbours at that time: 'Is not this the fast that I choose: to loose the bonds of injustice, to undo the thongs of the yoke, to let the oppressed go free, and to break every yoke? Is it not to share your bread with the hungry, and bring the homeless poor into your house; when you see the naked, to cover them, and not to hide yourself from your own kin?' The challenges may be different today, but the principle of having regard for your poor neighbour still stands.

One of the most powerful verses in the Bible is John 13:35: 'By this everyone will know that you are my disciples, if you have love for one another.' This issue is also addressed in Isaiah 58, where 'the pointing of the finger, the speaking of evil' is condemned among the children of Israel (v. 9). Is our church life distinctive by the love we have for one another? Are people attracted to the gospel because of the loving relationships they encounter?

Verses 13 and 14 talk about the importance of treating the sabbath day as God intended. Taking a sabbath day is perhaps the first thing that God did that we can imitate when he rested after creating the world (Genesis 2:2). The fourth commandment tells us to 'remember the sabbath day, and keep it holy' (Exodus 20:8). It is one way that the people of Israel demonstrated their adherence to their faith; it was a distinctive way of living, one which is still often followed in Judaism today. It is a day with perhaps a bit more time and space to encounter God, often with and through each other.

Guidelines

Our connectedness to God, ourselves, our neighbours and the earth is often worked out through spiritual disciplines. In a world where issues of loneliness, stewardship and mental health, among many others, have such an impact, spiritual disciplines can be part of the answer. How does our engagement in spiritual disciplines help to bring life in all its fullness to ourselves and others? How do our actions make a difference to the lives of others and witness, in action and or words, the kindness and love of God?

There are various ways of framing a rule and rhythm of life which can incorporate some of the practices discussed, but there are many other potential elements too, such as pilgrimage – an intentional journey away from the familiar – keeping a daily pattern of prayer, silent contemplation, social action and prophetic witness. Consider developing or reviewing your personal rhythm of life. Is there scope in your context to develop a corporate one? What might you include?

We can be conformed to or transformed by either God or the world (Romans 12:1–2). Spiritual disciplines play their part in this. With social media and online forums showing a growing interest in engaging in spiritual disciplines, it may be particularly relevant to consider the extent to which our engagement with these is conformational or transformational in the direction of God.

Using the Ignatian examen is a way of reflecting on our lives which complements these disciplines. I use these two questions, asking the Holy Spirit to guide me: Where/when did you find consolation/joy/life or feel alive/recharged/contentment? Where/when did you find desolation/death/draining/despair/frustration/sorrow (see Nash, 2006)? As I reflect on the answers to these questions, I find I bring to God the things that I need to, and I become more aware of the work of the Holy Spirit in my discipleship and growth to wholeness.

FURTHER READING

Dietrich Bonhoeffer, *Life Together* (SCM, 2015).

Justin Whitmel Earley, *The Common Rule: Habits of purpose for an age of distraction* (IVP, 2019).

Alan Hargrave, *Living Well: Finding a 'rule of life' to revitalise and sustain us* (SPCK, 2010).

Christopher Jamison, *Finding Sanctuary: Monastic steps for everyday life* (Wiedenfeld and Nicolson, 2006).

John Lane, *Timeless Simplicity: Creative living in a consumer society* (Green Books, 2001).

Sally Nash, *Sustaining Your Spirituality* (Grove Books, 2006).

Stephen Pattison, *Saving Face: Enfacement, shame, theology* (Routledge, 2016).

Andrew Roberts, *Holy Habits* (Malcolm Down Publishing, 2016).

Robert Schnase, *Five Practices of Fruitful Congregations* (revised edition, Abingdon, 2018).

Cate Williams, *Forest Church: Earthed perspectives on the gospel (Mission and Evangelism)* (Grove Books, 2019).

Death and the promise of new life

Lucy Peppiatt

At Easter time, we often tend to focus only on the stories in the Bible that lead directly to the crucifixion – the last few days of Jesus' life on earth. This can sometimes give us the wrong impression that the story of our salvation is only connected to the few days around Easter, the crucifixion and the resurrection of Jesus. To some extent, this is reinforced by the gospel accounts, which tend to focus more on the last few days of Jesus' life than his entire life before that. But it isn't only Jesus' death and resurrection that tell us about how God came to save humanity. It is the whole of Jesus' life that gives us a window into the nature of God, what he has done for us in Jesus, and why and how he came to save us.

The cross is the culmination and centre of God's work in the world, but how God the Son submits himself to this path of life and death also tells us about who God is, how he works and what we mean to him. In our second week of notes we will celebrate the reality and the excitement of the bodily resurrection of Jesus Christ. For three days the disciples must have lived with the despair of Jesus' death, the trauma of the cruelty they had witnessed, the shattering of their hopes and dreams. We can't imagine what those days were like and how deep their pain was at losing not just a close friend, but also a brother, a son, a leader and a comforter. They must, at times, have felt that they were on the cusp of victory for the Jewish nation, only for it to be snatched from them. Here they were, with their king mocked for all to see, their dreams in tatters, their hearts broken.

But this wasn't the end of the story. Everything that Jesus had promised was about to come true. The new era was about to begin. They were going to see and know something that would change the very fabric of their beings. If their world had lurched sickeningly into darkness on Good Friday, it was about to burst into glorious light, more glorious than they could have ever imagined.

Unless otherwise stated, Bible quotations are taken from the NRSV.

1 The image of the invisible God

John 1:1–18

At the beginning of time, God the Father, Son and Holy Spirit knew that the Son was going to come to earth in the form of a servant, a humble man, who was going to live a life just like ours and yet without sin (Hebrews 2:17–18). This man, Jesus of Nazareth, was going to live and die as a human being, all the while he was still God. The Son is the image of the invisible God, and yet when he comes to earth we find that this image is just like us. He is made in our image – he literally looks like one of us.

At the same time, he is in the world revealing God to those around him. Who would have thought that the greatest revelation of God would come in the form of something that looks just like us? You would have thought it would be far more spectacular than that. There are so many things that the incarnation tells us about God and about ourselves. It tells us that God loves humans so much that he unites himself to humanity. God the Son, who is with God and is God, is the one who is suited to assume human flesh. This human existence is not a cloak hiding his divinity, but a union of the human and the divine in one person, while the human remains fully human and the divine remains fully divine.

The means by which God sheds his greatest light into the world is through a human form in the person of Jesus. Although the Son was there at creation and the world was made through him, he then came to the world he made and took part in every aspect of it. He lived among us. It is through this that we see the glory of God. But it is also through this that he committed himself to death, because it is only in human flesh that he could die. He was God from God and light from light, and yet once he was united to human flesh, his life had to go the way of all flesh. He had to suffer and die. The story we dwell on at Easter is why he had to die a shameful death, the death of the outcast and sinner, when he himself had done nothing wrong.

2 The good news!

Mark begins: 'The beginning of the good news of Jesus Christ, the Son of God!' I added in the exclamation mark, as the statement sounds like a fantastic announcement. The beginning of the good news for the world in Mark's gospel is not the birth of Jesus, but his baptism. It begins with John the Baptiser announcing the imminent arrival of the Messiah: 'Prepare the way of the Lord' (v. 3). John began baptising people with a baptism of repentance. The way for the people to prepare for Jesus was repentance in the wilderness, confessing their sins, submitting to the cleansing of John's baptism and waiting for the revealing of the Messiah. John promises that this one who is more powerful than he will baptise with the Holy Spirit, a sign of the power and presence of God. Jesus presents himself first to be baptised by John.

In Matthew's gospel, John protests, 'I need to be baptised by you, and do you come to me?', but Jesus answers, 'Let it be so now; for it is proper for us in this way to fulfil all righteousness' (Matthew 3:14–15). We know that Jesus himself was without sin, and yet Paul tells us that he came to earth 'in the likeness of sinful flesh' (Romans 8:3). It was this coming in the likeness of sinful flesh, in an existence just like ours, that made him committed not just to a human life, but a human death. What had begun at his incarnation begins to be played out in front of us as he arrives to begin his public ministry.

Jesus' baptism symbolises and embodies his unswerving commitment to taking the place of sinful humanity and to stand in our stead. He fulfils God's righteousness by taking the judgement that is meant for us upon himself. But as he does so, we find that he is marked with an equally unswerving commitment of the Father towards the Son. God's voice is heard, 'You are my Son, the Beloved; with you I am well pleased' (v. 11). Many were going to have occasion to doubt the truth of these words as Jesus determined to head for the cross. Even he, in his fully human state, was going to suffer the deepest sense of human alienation from God. And yet through it all, these words were going to be over him: the Beloved Son in whom God dwells eternally.

3 God made man

Luke 7:36–50

The Son submits himself to a fully human existence. At first he is born as a baby, having grown in a woman's womb. He suffers the uncleanness (both ritual and real) of childbirth. He grows up and begins his public ministry, first submitting himself to a baptism of repentance when he has nothing of which to repent. He then repents on behalf of humanity, in whose form he now exists. He experiences the cleansing of water and the rising again to receive the baptism of the Holy Spirit, in whose power he would heal the sick, deliver the oppressed, save the lost and go eventually to his death. And in this story, he submits himself to another anointing. The fully divine Son in his human existence allows what is 'sinful' to come near: far too close for comfort, in fact!

Simon the Pharisee criticises Jesus for letting this sinful woman touch him. In the parallel story of anointing in Matthew 26:6–13, the disciples become angry, and in the Marcan version, his disciples scold *her* (Mark 14:3–9). In all of the stories, the gesture is too extravagant, too shameful, too hard to watch. This woman, who wastes far too much expensive oil on the one who has saved her and loved her, brings shame on herself and him. And yet Jesus resists this shame, knowing that her gesture is a recognition by her of who he is and what he is destined for.

In our account in Luke, this is the story of the forgiveness of the woman's sins. Jesus has authority to forgive sins. In Matthew's account, Jesus says that the woman is preparing his body for burial, looking ahead to his death. Throughout his ministry, Jesus tries to teach his disciples that he has come to suffer and to die, but most of the time they can't understand this. We don't know if this woman knows that Jesus is going to die, but she knows that he has saved her. She falls at his feet in love and worship. She can't stop kissing his feet. She bathes them and dries them with her hair. She anoints him with oil.

In the two anointing stories from yesterday and today, Jesus first receives the adoration of the Father as the beloved Son as he is anointed with the Holy Spirit; in this second one, he receives the anointing of a sinful woman, the one who clings to him in adoration and gratitude. And it is for this sinner and all who sin and fall short of the glory of God that he agrees to go to the cross.

4 Setting the people free

Luke 22:7–23

In this scene at the Passover, Jesus is in the final preparations before his death. In this Passover meal, he celebrates the exodus with his disciples, remembering how God delivered his people out of slavery in Egypt and led them into the promised land. In the supper, they remember the promises of God for the liberation of his people. This must have been all the more poignant as they met there in an occupied land, under the oppression and rule of a foreign nation in the land that rightfully belonged to them. Liberation must never have been very far from their thoughts. As he speaks, Jesus makes it sound as if this longed-for liberation is near. He tells them that he won't eat again of the Passover until the Passover is fulfilled again in the kingdom of God. This sounds as if liberation is imminent – the power of God manifest to set them free.

They didn't realise, however, that he was talking about his death on the cross, the final and ultimate sacrifice. This was going to be the act of God that would set them free. Jesus gives them the cup of wine to signify the blood that would be spilt and the bread to signify his body that would be broken for them. Without his commitment to a human life, Jesus would never have had a body, a body that could be stripped, flogged and crucified in a terrible, torturous, horrifying death. He would never have had a body that could suffer pain and agony, fear, panic and the suffocation of a crucifixion. And yet it's through this body that he establishes the new covenant. It's through this body that we can take part in his life. He tells his disciples in John 6:53–55, 'Very truly, I tell you, unless you eat the flesh of the Son of Man and drink his blood, you have no life in you. Those who eat my flesh and drink my blood have eternal life, and I will raise them up on the last day; for my flesh is true food and my blood is true drink.'

Each time we take Communion together, we remember again the sacrifice of Jesus on the cross to set us free, liberated not always from the earthly rulers that run the world, but from the power of sin and guilt, shame and condemnation, and from the principalities and powers behind them. This is the entry into the new covenant and the new kingdom, a kingdom where we too experience the deep love of God the Father as we are reconciled with him. He took on a body like ours so that he could heal our earthly existence as well as give us the promise of wholeness to come.

5 Not my will but yours

Jesus is nearing his death, and he goes to pray. It's here in the garden that we see how truly human Jesus is. Knowing what lies ahead in the immediate days, he goes to his Father, asking if this cup might be taken from him. Like all of us in this life, he does not want to suffer and die. He has a strong instinct to live. People often wonder how Jesus seems to have a will that is different from the Father. If he is also divine, why doesn't he have the same will? How come it seems as if he is merely human here?

We know that Jesus had two natures: one fully human and one fully divine. And with these two natures, he had corresponding wills. He had a human will and a divine will, and in his earthly life he had committed to living as we live and so he functioned in his humanity. Here we see his human will and how he always willed in line with the Father, even in his human frailty. This is how he knew exactly what it was like to live a human life. As he willed to do the Father's willing, the Spirit comforted him, guarded him, filled him and interceded with him and for him with groans too deep for words. Jesus in the garden was in agony because he had submitted himself to a human life. But Hebrews 12:2 says that he endured the cross 'for the sake of the joy that was set before him'. Even in his human life, the Son has a revelation of what God is going to do for him and through him, and this carries him through his terrible trial.

The disciples are weak and cannot stand by him. They fall asleep. There's something so terribly lonely about this scene. In Matthew's gospel Jesus says to his disciples, 'Could you not stay awake with me one hour?' (Matthew 26:40). But despite their failure to support and comfort him, Jesus goes to his death for them. God saves us in our weakness. When God formed the covenant with Abraham, Abraham slept while God passed through the sacrificed animals (Genesis 15:9–20). While Jesus' disciples sleep, he prepares to pass through the death that by right belongs to them and to us, and to become the perfect sacrifice himself.

6 King of the Jews and king of the cosmos

Having been tried in a mock trial and falsely accused, Jesus is led to his death. The innocent one dies a criminal's death. Crucifixion is a horrific death associated with slaves and rebels. It was so awful that even the Romans didn't like to speak about it. It was shameful beyond belief and here he is, crucified alongside two criminals. Jesus had a body that was frail and vulnerable just like ours. He had a body that was stripped, tortured, spat on, stared at and mocked. But it was this body that he had taken on for our sake that meant he could be alongside broken humanity, identified as he was with the criminals on his right and on his left. Where he should have been flanked by angels, surrounded with glory and light, here he is hung on a cross in shame and humility, identifying himself with the worst of humanity and the worst of conditions that a human can be in.

This was the king of the Jews and the king of the cosmos displaying his deep love for humanity. Those who stand in front of him mock him, but out of his pain, he cries out to his Father to forgive them, to release them from eternal judgement. One of the men beside him sees that Jesus, as the innocent one, does not deserve a criminal's death. 'Jesus, remember me when you come into your kingdom,' he says, and Jesus replies, 'Truly I tell you, today you will be with me in Paradise' (vv. 42–43). Jesus' compassion and forgiveness pours out of him even as he is dying.

Guidelines

This Easter, take time to reflect on what it means for Jesus to be 'fully human'. The early church fathers wrote, 'He became like us so that we could become like him.' He has taken all the sin, pain, brokenness and unforgiveness of the world on to his shoulders, and it has been crucified with him so that we can be free.

Think about:

- The importance of Jesus' having a body and what that means for our bodies.
- The love of God poured out on Jesus that is the same love poured into our hearts by the Holy Spirit.
- The way he accepts our worship when we come to him just as we are.
- The way he is prepared to die for us when we have nothing to give him and even though we are fast asleep.
- His forgiveness, compassion and care even to the point of death.

1 He is not here: he is risen!

Matthew 28:1–20

In this account (compare Luke 24:1–12), we're told that Mary Magdalene and the other Mary went to see the tomb. In other accounts of the women's visit, there is a larger group of women and they go to anoint his body. Here the women are present when they experience a great earthquake and see the angel of the Lord descend from heaven to roll back the stone. The angel proclaims, 'He is not here; for he has been raised, as he said' (v. 6). He invites them to come and see. I love this phrase 'as he said'. Everything Jesus promised has happened up until now, so all his promises are going to come to pass – it is just as he said. So often we find ourselves waiting for God's promises to be fulfilled. We feel the darkness of disappointment and even despair as we feel everything we have longed for has been dashed. The resurrection of Jesus gives us hope that everything God has promised will one day be fulfilled. It will be as he has said. Every tear will be wiped away and all will be well, even if the times now are dark.

In this story, the amazing news that the women hear from the angel excites them with fear and joy! This is not surprising, as their adrenalin levels must have been very high. Whatever will happen next? They are on their way, running to find the disciples, when suddenly Jesus meets them. Imagine the exhilaration that they felt on seeing him again – alive! They fall at his feet and worship him. He too tells them not to be afraid, but to go and tell the disciples. There is a wonderful sense of energy and excitement about the resurrection stories. In this one, we see how the resurrection is the foundation of the Christian faith and the beginning of calling on the church to 'go' and 'tell'.

As Paul says, if Christ has not been raised, our faith is in vain (1 Corinthians 15:14); but our faith in God's promises is not in vain, so we are commissioned to go and tell the world the good news. There is a strange verse at the end of Matthew 28 where we read, 'but some doubted'. We have no idea for how long they doubted, but we know that not everyone got the full revelation all at once. For some it is a process. This should encourage us as we share the good news. We are called to 'go', but the outcome is in God's hands and not ours.

2 Worshipping Thomas

The most famous story of someone doubting is the story of Thomas, who even ended up being identified by his doubt – 'doubting Thomas'! This is a bit unfair, as even though he doubts, by the end of the story he falls down and worships Jesus as Lord. In the end he is 'believing Thomas' or 'worshipping Thomas'. Thomas was a man who wanted to see for himself, to know for himself. I'm sure many people identify with this. Thomas wasn't prepared to take in this phenomenal news just on the hearsay of his friends. Surely that is fair enough. How can you trust a group of grieving friends not to be susceptible to wish fulfilment? Also how did they know it was real and not a vision? He says to his friends, 'Unless I see the mark of the nails in his hands, and put my finger in the mark of the nails and my hand in his side, I will not believe' (v. 25). That's a very specific condition.

A week later, we find that Jesus had been listening all along to Thomas' conversation with the other disciples, and he decides to answer Thomas' prayer. What I love about this story is the way that we see, in Jesus' response to Thomas, what kind of God we worship. I think the turning point for Thomas was not that Jesus walked through the door and was suddenly there with them, but that he showed Thomas that he'd been listening all along, he'd heard his doubt, he knew what he needed and he was willing to offer that to him. It was this knowledge and love of him as a person that convinced Thomas that he was in the presence of God, a God who knew his every thought, his every doubt, his every worry, and who had the grace and compassion to appear just to him so that he too would believe.

I hear many stories of people who end up praying a prayer like Thomas'. *Unless I see this, hear this, feel this, I won't be able to believe.* God is so gracious, and he answers those prayers. We shouldn't discourage those around us if they tell us that they need to see or know something specific in order not to doubt, but to believe. If we know people like Thomas, maybe we should encourage them to ask Jesus to reveal himself to them as they want to see him, and trust that he will.

3 Mary meets the rabbi

This version of the resurrection begins with Mary Magdalene coming to the tomb 'while it was still dark'. It must have been very early in the morning. She sees the stone has been removed and so runs to tell Peter and another disciple. They too run to the tomb, although the second disciple outruns Peter. He stops though at the entrance and doesn't enter the tomb. This reminds us of the 'fear' of the women on hearing Jesus is raised from the dead. We tend to think of Peter as a bit of a hothead, and here he behaves according to type. He charges past his friends and runs into the tomb. Peter sees the linen burial wrappers lying there empty, and they both believe that Jesus is not dead, but it's unclear at this stage what exactly they believe beyond that. As a bit of an anticlimax, John tells us they just go home.

We often find in the gospels that women are portrayed as more faithful than the men. Mary stays, weeping outside the tomb. It is she that sees the angels, not the men. They ask her why she is weeping, and her response is that she believes that someone has taken Jesus' body and put it somewhere else. She then turns and sees a man. He asks her why she is weeping, and she tells him. Jesus then says her name, 'Mary.' At this, she turns to him and calls him a familiar name, the one she has always used for him, 'Rabbouni', Rabbi in Hebrew. It appears that she must have rushed to hug him or to embrace him in some way, as Jesus says to her, 'Do not hold on to me.' This sounds strange to us, because we know from other accounts of the resurrection that he allowed himself to be touched. It seems that what he meant by this was that she shouldn't cling to him or try to hold him in a way that wouldn't allow her to let him go. He knew that he was going to ascend and leave them again and only be present with them through the presence of the Spirit. They would no longer have him with them. He tells her to warn the others (her brothers) that he would ascend. Mary goes and announces, 'I have seen the Lord' (v. 18).

4 Abundant resurrection life

John 21:1–14

It seems in most of the resurrection appearances that the people who saw Jesus didn't recognise him straight away. We're not told why this is the case. We don't know whether it was because Jesus looked different from how he had looked in life before his death or because they weren't expecting to see him and so couldn't compute what was in front of them. In this story, we find seven of the disciples by the Sea of Tiberias setting out on a fishing trip. They were out all night and caught nothing. Jesus is standing on the shore as day breaks, but they don't recognise him. He instructs them where to cast their nets, and they catch more than they can handle.

This story is similar to another story that we have in Luke 5:1–11, in which Simon Peter, James and John had been fishing all night and had caught nothing. Back then Jesus told them where to cast their nets and the same thing happened – a great haul of fish filled both boats! Peter fell at Jesus' feet saying, 'Go away from me, Lord, for I am a sinful man!' (Luke 5:8). It's a powerful story. So when the same thing happens here in a different setting, Peter immediately would have known that this was Jesus. 'It is the Lord!' he cries out and is so excited that he throws on some clothes and leaps into the water, swimming towards him.

Peter's enthusiasm here is palpable. It's a wonderful, joyous story. People often notice that there is an unusual detail here, where John records the number of fish as 153. This symbolises abundance and would have reminded the disciples of Jesus' promise that he was going to make them fishers of people. This story and the story in Luke tell us that they and we can't do that on our own. We have to hear God's voice telling us where to cast our nets and simply obey him. Some of us feel as if we have been fishing all night and caught nothing. But finding fish is the Lord's task. Our task is just to keep fishing. The Lord can surprise us, showing up at any time and telling us where to find an abundant haul.

5 Jesus: hard to recognise

Luke 24:13–27

In this passage there are two disciples walking on the road to Emmaus from Jerusalem. It's another story in which Jesus' disciples don't recognise him at first and he has to do something in front of them to trigger their memory and comprehension. Here it is even stranger than our last story, as these disciples are right next to him, walking and talking, and not at a distance. We're told that Cleopas is travelling with another. It's amazing how many commentators and preachers assume that these were two men. It is more likely to be Cleopas and his wife.

While they are talking about everything that has just happened, and the distressing scenes that they have witnessed, Jesus joins them, seemingly out of nowhere. They are despondent, sharing with this stranger how they had hoped that Jesus was the one to redeem Israel, but now their hopes appear to have been dashed. What is even stranger about this story is that these two disciples have begun to hear rumours about Jesus' rising from the dead, but they still are slow to believe. Jesus rebukes them because of it.

Here is another instance of the 'doubting Thomas' syndrome, and again Jesus helps them to see what they cannot see on their own. For these disciples, he opens up the scriptures to them, explaining how what has happened had been foretold in the scriptures and all pointed to him. But they still don't see.

6 'Were not our hearts burning within us?'

Luke 24:28–43

After Jesus has explained everything to Cleopas and the other disciple in the scriptures and they still haven't understood that it is him, it seems that Jesus makes the decision to leave them. But they urge him to stay and eat with them. It is as he takes the bread, blesses it and breaks it that they suddenly recognise Jesus for who he is. The breaking and blessing of bread is something that he would have done with them so often. At that moment, he disappears, leaving them in awe and wonder.

Looking back, they realise that they had felt the power of his presence as he had unfolded the scriptures to them on the road. 'Were not our hearts burning within us?' they ask (v. 32). They get up and return to Jerusalem, excited by what has happened. They find the disciples and their companions, and the excitement runs through the whole story – 'The Lord has risen indeed!' (v. 34). These stories tell us something very deep about how revelation comes to people. These are people who knew Jesus, who had walked with him, eaten with him, travelled with him, listened to him and learned from him – and still they are slow to see and understand.

We live in a culture that is slow to understand who Jesus is. Some people are happy to be around Christians, but it takes a long time until they are happy to ask Jesus to come in and eat with them. Sometimes they've come to church, heard the scriptures and spent time in his presence, but still they don't get to the point where they can see. This story encourages us that revelation is a process. It can take time, and often people only realise in hindsight how the Holy Spirit was at work in their lives all along.

Guidelines

At this Easter time, take some time to meditate on the variety of resurrection stories. Place yourself at the scene and imagine how you would feel if it were you.

- Ask God to reveal the truth of the resurrected Jesus to you all over again.
- Talk to friends and ask them what one thing would convince them that Jesus was real.
- Pray for the people you know who have walked with Jesus, met him, maybe even heard some of his teaching, but haven't asked him to stay and eat. Pray that they will get to the point where they can do this and that he will reveal himself to them.
- Trust that God is working in your friends and family by his Spirit to reveal who he is in Jesus Christ.

FURTHER READING

Richard Bauckham, *Jesus and the Eyewitnesses: The gospels as eyewitness testimony* (Eerdmans, 2008).

Colin E. Gunton, *The Christian Faith: An introduction to Christian doctrine* (Blackwell Publishing, 2002).

Stanley Hauerwas, *Cross-Shattered Christ: Meditations on the seven last words* (Darton, Longman and Todd, 2004).

Marianne Meye Thompson, *God of the Gospel of John* (Eerdmans, 2001).

Jean Vanier, *Becoming Human* (Darton, Longman and Todd, 1999).

Job

Alec Gilmore

To the casual reader Job is a good story. Too much to read at one sitting, perhaps, but try reading chapters 1—3, skipping lightly through 4—37, reading 38—41 more carefully and then reading every word of 42. Traditionally Job is interpreted as a faithful believer, well blessed with this world's goods, an ideal family and a good reputation, who one day loses everything and challenges God with injustice, asking, why me? It's hardly a precursor to the Protestant work ethic (be faithful and work hard and you will prosper), but it is still quarried by many of that persuasion. Overall the principle has legs, until one day a man sticks his head above the parapet and says, 'Hang on! I always believed and practised that, but today it no longer works.' That man is Job.

'Satan' not then having arrived on the scene, the original text presupposes an 'adversary' (lit. 'accuser'), who conceives a cunning plan to discredit the traditional doctrine. Job, caught in the crossfire, struggles to find a solution, helped (perhaps?) by three friends, until despair drives him to head-to-head confrontation with Yahweh, with surprising results.

Interpretations of Job are many, ranging from a rebellious protest against the doctrine of innocent suffering to patient endurance (in the early church), the reliability of divine justice (Calvin) and the human condition (Voltaire), overlooking that Job's battle is not so much with God as with a particularly limited but widespread understanding of God, but the major emphasis has almost always fallen on Job. *His* book. *His* story. So what happens if we shift the focus from Job to his friends, who came to 'console and comfort' (2:11)? What do they say and do, and with what result?

Divine justice is hardly popular for today's preachers, but approaching it from a different angle may uncover a Job for the 21st century. The story is timeless. We all know that moment when life tumbles in and we need a friend, and we all have friends who at some point may need us. Walking in Job's shoes, or trying on the shoes of his friends, can help us to a richer understanding of what both parties were going through, providing fresh insight today for friend and victim.

Unless otherwise stated, Bible quotations are taken from the NRSV.

1 A story and a problem

Try to read this story as if it were today, not yesterday. Separate the wood (the underlying issues of eternal significance) from the trees (the details that help us to get there). Try to enter into the experience of those who first heard it, not analysing it, but rather, like a piece of music, taking it as a whole and enjoying it.

First, Job and his world. Here is a man who lives in something of a fantasy world not unlike the American Dream. It is the only world he has ever known. He imbibed it with his mother's milk, never questioned it and practised it with unswerving devotion, carefully covering not only his own back but that of his children, even with no evidence to justify it, and it had served him well. So what happens when this world collapses? Try to get inside Job's experience. Wear his shoes. What are his family going to think… his friends going to say… or the wider community going to whisper? And where can he turn for help?

Second, his friends. The Hebrew word (usually translated 'friend') lends itself to other translations, so there is no need to confine your thinking to personal friends. Think of them simply as 'companions' or 'fellow-travellers'; this is helped by the fact that we know nothing of their background. What is clear, however, is that they come from the same tradition, united by a common purpose to 'comfort and console'. And they start well – they simply sit in silence and hold his hand.

Third, the reaction. When the silence gets too much for Job, he blows his top, and they quickly join in the fray. What he says is of little substance. Suddenly finding himself in a situation of which he has no experience, he just wants his life back – not silence, not comfort, not even explanations. He wants that world of fairness and justice he thought he had always lived in, and if he were to meet Yahweh, that is clearly what he would tell him. But the friends are not listening. They too are out of their depth. Notice how the exchanges flow.

2 That's life (Eliphaz)

Eliphaz, first out of the blocks, knows the theory (black and white) and will defend it to the death. His counselling skills, however, are somewhat limited, and he doesn't get off to the best start as he wades in at the deep end with a bit of straight talking, telling Job to take his own medicine (4:1–11). Then comes the textbook: good people don't suffer; the rest get what they deserve. Come to think of it, nobody can be truly innocent in the eyes of God, and most of our problems are of our own making. That's life (4:12—5:7). Finally, the remedy: if I were you, I would pray about it. God is a great disciplinarian; he may hurt, but he will always heal (5:8–27). There is nothing wrong with the sentiments in his day and generation, but he hasn't even begun to listen. He doesn't get it, and Job is not helped.

Job is needled – slightly. If only it were that simple. He knows all that as well as they do. He has built his life on it, and (yes) he has preached it. His problem is that *personal experience is in conflict with belief*. Why? And what next? Eliphaz has not even tried to grasp the depth and reality of Job's problem, let alone explanations, but has no doubt about the answers. Job believes God alone can help, but God seems no longer to be on hand, leaving him an embarrassment to his friends, who are unable to tell him where he has gone wrong. He is willing to learn but doubts their ability to teach.

So here is a client, intelligent, 'successful' and hitherto more than capable of handling his life, suddenly finding himself in entirely unfamiliar territory. Yet it is hardly new. Job apparently has already counselled others in similar circumstances. What is new is that it has never before happened to *him*, and now he is discovering that none of his answers, solutions or explanations work. He can't think why, nor can his close friends who have shared his life, as solipsism once again takes over until self-pity is interrupted by Bildad.

3 This is God (Bildad)

Like many of our contemporaries, unfamiliar with Jesus, who preached a different gospel ('neither do I condemn you'; see John 8:11), Bildad must be judged by the traditions of his faith and day, and when confronted by acute suffering or stress his approach is still all too familiar today. But whereas Eliphaz is content to *proclaim* the dogma, Bildad sets out to *defend* it.

Bildad's 'comfort' is 'stop moaning and pull yourself together'. If you do wrong, you will pay the price; if not, you have nothing to worry about. That is God, and that is how divine justice works. All history knows it. God will never reject a faithful person, nor will he have any truck with wrongdoers other than their just punishment. What you can't do is accuse God of injustice. If goodness produces good results and wrongdoing bad, that is either self-imposed or divine justice. That is Bildad. That is his view of God; to feel the force of it, sit where Job sits or think of somebody who does.

Alternatively, ask yourself what Job hears. Job wants to know how to challenge the ways of God (vv. 3, 11–12). But Bildad's God is unchallengeable – too big and too powerful. He crushes Job with a tempest (9:17), holds all the cards (9:19) and leaves Job feeling boxed in (9:29); the contest is unequal (9:32). In a battle with that God, Job hasn't got a chance. If Job is wicked, he suffers; even if he isn't, he still cannot face his friends because all they do is intensify residual guilt as a result of traditional teaching and training (9:15–18).

Bildad, like Eliphaz, just doesn't understand. Either he has never been down this road or cannot recognise it sufficiently to help someone who has. Bildad's God of justice and fairness (8:5–9) prohibits his ability to help.

All is not lost, however. Job's ultimate despair (chapter 10) is less self-centred. You begin to feel him standing up and getting the gloves off. Is he beginning to see that his problem is not so much God as their incipient interpretations of God?

4 Stop worrying (Zophar)

Zophar, a very different character, loses patience. Coming from the same stable, he is well aware of the questions and the arguments, but doesn't let them get to him. He has learned to live with them. God knows best. God is just and Job is probably getting less than he deserves (11:6). The issue is not worth the candle. Best to put your life in order; you will soon get over it and all will be well. Look at it this way: instead of impugning God's justice, try seeking God's help to take a fresh look at your lifestyle and find peace (11:13–19). Sounds rather like a bad Agony Aunt. Zophar is not unlike Bildad, but on a different basis (Bildad on doctrinal grounds, Zophar coldly rational), and that is enough to spark Job to a counter-attack.

Having your beliefs challenged is one thing; being patronised or not being treated seriously ('a laughing-stock', v. 4) is another. Job is as well informed as they are, and by their attitudes they are trivialising the issue. If that is the best they can do, he will appeal to a higher court, as Job resumes the pedestal on which he has lived all his life to teach them a thing or two.

He invites them to look at nature. In their culture, nature and God were very closely connected, and though Job does not spell out precisely the details or what nature teaches us, a little imagination might suggest that the all-powerful God may be in control but not everything always runs as smoothly as we might expect. 'Nature red in tooth and claw' comes to mind. Or (if God really is all-powerful) might Job be suggesting that God has to be held responsible for the unfairness and inequality of life? If so, what have they to say to that?

In righteous anger, Job accuses his friends of whitewash and lies. If their previous meanderings are the best they can do, they would be wiser to say nothing, leave him alone and let him get on with his quest. Self-confidence gives him hope that he will be vindicated.

5 Lament of a laughing stock (Eliphaz 2)

Job 16:11–22

Job's explosion triggers something in Eliphaz. If round one was the Agony Aunt, round two reads more like 'Listen to me, sunshine!' (15:17–35). Eliphaz may be down, but he is not out. They are not getting anywhere. Having dismissed words as 'unprofitable' (15:3), Eliphaz proceeds to utter more, accusing Job of using protest to detract from traditional religious experience, dubbing it 'the tongue of the crafty' (15:4–5). He then charges Job with venting his wrath on his friends because he cannot get at God, like a man who picks a quarrel with the church so that he can get out.

Then, as if that were not offensive enough, Eliphaz challenges Job on three points: what training has he ever had (instilling inferiority); is he too young to understand what has always been handed down (dubbing him a rebel); and what on earth is biting him to behave like this (diverting the conversation from Job's problem which they don't want to talk about) (15:7–16). Finally, with no evidence for his assertions, he tries to frighten Job with the lot of the wicked (deep down they are unhappy), a doctrine of which Job is well aware, doesn't question and is bright enough to see its irrelevance (15:17–35).

In response, Job chooses to reverse the role. He's heard it all before, and if he were in their shoes (though there is no sign that *they* have ever felt to be in *his*) he could say all they are saying, but so what? It just wouldn't help. So, dreadfully abandoned by his friends, he sometimes even feels abandoned by God and given over to the ungodly in a crisis where he needs God and the godly more than ever (vv. 11–22).

Avoid getting too involved in what Job *says*. Reflect rather on what he *feels*. Genuinely struggling with an unusual experience, which his friends neither understand nor know how to handle or discuss, he feels treated like a 'weirdo' or a 'nutcase'. Embarrassed and shattered by what has happened, he is afraid to speak; nobody will believe him and some will even hold him responsible.

6 Not their line (Bildad 2)

First time round, Bildad seemed content to play it cool and with a straight bat. His counselling skills are hardly fit for purpose, but as a good friend he might have asked a few questions, tried to suss out the situation and clarify what exactly was bugging Job. But no. Bildad is not that kind of friend. He knows why he is there, what he has to do and how best to do it. This time, having sat through the other exchanges, Bildad is impatient and easily rattled (18:1–4). He resorts to character assassination: Job is just being unreasonable. He's not listening to what they keep trying to tell him. Does he not hear or is he stubborn? Or has the penny not dropped for Bildad that it is they who are missing the point and addressing the wrong question? Safer to take a different line – the fear of God (18:5–21).

Meanwhile, a tormented man and now the victim of a personal attack, Job holds himself together well and tries to explain. God has put him in the wrong, and he needs help to get back on course in his quest for divine fairness and justice. What can be wrong with that, and what has Bildad to offer? On the surface, for Job, it is an intellectual or doctrinal issue, but since Bildad and his colleagues have no answer to that, they might at least have asked him why it mattered so much and what difference it made to his life. After all, many others had had similar experiences (if not so extreme) and they had coped. Why couldn't he?

Sensitive to the impasse, Job tries to move on a stage. This is not just a doctrinal issue. There are personal consequences; he has lost the confidence and trust of his family, his colleagues, his staff and his friends (especially the three of them). But why? What has he done wrong to alienate a whole community? He might have expected at least one of them to ask him about this. But no. That's not their line. Do they really want to comfort Job? Probably not, but they do want to defend the dogma.

Guidelines

- What does the list of offences Job has never committed (31:5–34) tell us about him?

- Which of the friends do you think was most (or least) helpful? Focus on one point which merits further reflection when next confronted with a friend's crisis situation.

- In the light of 4:1–6, think of a doctor facing a serious operation or a marriage counsellor confronting the break-up of their own marriage. Reflect on the difference between handling other people's problems and your own, or ponder Job's feelings alongside that of any victim of assault or other similar personal crisis.

- Recall a situation when you felt like Job or were called in to help someone experiencing Job's sense of frustration and isolation. Jot down briefly what you said and what questions you might have asked but didn't. Compare your attitude and responses to those of Job and his friends.

- At what point does help for a friend switch from commitment to your friend to commitment to your argument?

1 Job spots an opening (Zophar 2)

Job 21:7-34

Feeling insulted, Zophar plays the hurt card, though what he offers is barely different from Bildad part 2 (the wicked suffer, have a bad time and are unhappy). By now, the reader must be wondering: surely they know that not all the faithful prosper nor are all wrongdoers miserable. How can they churn out such platitudes totally isolated from reality? But wait. This very question is emerging in Job's consciousness. Time to take the battle to 'the comforters'. *His* house has collapsed like a pack of cards. Time to blow down Zophar's pack and extinguish any flicker of light that might be there.

Do they not know that the wicked live to a ripe old age (v. 7)? Their houses are safe, their cattle breed successfully, their children mature and enjoy music and dancing. Their message to God is 'Leave us alone'. So what is the point of faithfulness… and so on, until he blows a gasket with verse 34.

Until now, Eliphaz (with his doctrine) and Bildad (with his rationale) have kept the conversation in their comfort zone with nothing fresh to offer. This time round, Zophar's cool and practical logic touches a nerve and blows the lid off. What is said is secondary, but ponder what it says about the people who say it. Zophar, remember, is the 'friend' who has learned to live with the complexities he can't handle, but he is sufficiently detached not to be troubled by them. Maybe Job could do the same. It doesn't work, but for the first time it gives Job the opportunity to open up.

Job is thoughtful, not afraid to ask tough questions and needs someone to tango with him. The friends are not. They don't understand. They don't like it. They are not too keen on him breaking ranks, and that is the crucial difference between them. Had the friends probed a little as to what was getting Job so agitated, they might have discovered that it was because, stripped of everything he lived by, he had experienced how others live. Without that, the friends were ill-equipped to help; all their ramblings were in vain and, if anything, counterproductive. Time to listen.

2 A last throw of the dice (Eliphaz 3)

Job 22:1–11

After Job's outburst the genie is out. Pandora's Box has blown open. The character of the friends emerges. Bildad's cool, rational approach cuts no ice but chills the victim. Zophar tried as best he could, but when he got nowhere he sought refuge in 'see-how-much-your-attitude-hurts-me'. Eliphaz will never give up and goes for the jugular. Job's problem is the failure to confront his wickedness. Time for a quiet sermonette on repentance (22:21–30), and if Job thinks (as he does) that he has nothing to repent, Eliphaz will tell him. Never trifle with 'an Eliphaz' – he knows he is right and can get nasty if crossed. Frightening 'the sinner' with the flames of hell didn't begin yesterday.

But how realistic are the flames? With no evidence, it is difficult to say. Today, you might say Job has sinned in that he is part of a sinful community, but it would be difficult to establish that in this text, time and culture, and even if it were true it would hardly be the moment to embark on it to someone in crisis. Job is no fool and would not be where he is if he could be so easily put off. Job still cherishes his faith in God's fairness, if only he could get through to him.

What his friends miss is that there is more to life than 'answers', certainly than the slick traditional ones on offer. Job simply wants to meet God, argue his case, hear what God has to say and discover what God wants of him. He is a seeker, not a problem case looking for a solution. He knows his God would 'give heed' to him (23:4). What he wants is a face-to-face encounter. Unfortunately he can't find him, and his friends can hardly be blamed if they cannot deliver, but failing that he might have been better served if only he could meet one of God's humble assistants: somebody sympathetic, willing to listen and talk through the problem. Who knows? That way he might have found the God he was seeking. Certainly better than three friends with fixed positions, personal experiences and beginners' textbook answers.

3 Oh, for the glory days!

Job's summing up 'for the defence' takes him back to the past: days when the sun shone and the family worshipped him; how he helped the poor and anticipated a great old age, as people hung on his every word.

Whether this is to teach his friends what they don't know, to remind them what they seem to have forgotten or simply daydreaming or fantasising depends on how you read it. One way is to see it as a summary of what in extremis matters to Job and then ask yourself what is missing.

Did family and friends matter more for the warm feeling they gave *him* than for what he gave *them*? Did their withdrawal and silence when he appeared signify respect or fear, and did Job ever question which? Think of a tough manager suddenly turning up at the coal face, and notice that now when Job gets their attention it is the wrong sort (chapter 30). And might the fact that none of them fall over themselves to come to his aid say something about the relationship and (worse) how Job really feels about them?

On one reading Job comes across as a very self-centred man. As long as everything went well and ministered to his ego, all was fine. When it didn't, the question was not, 'Where have I gone wrong?' but, 'What has gone wrong with God?' Perhaps what we see here is that the 'god' he had pinned his life to is too small, and when it let him down he had nothing, few friends and nowhere to go. If so, he needs somebody to open his eyes, but very gently. He is a wounded man, and his three friends are not helping.

Job may have believed all the right things, done all the right things and avoided all the wrong things, but closer examination of his self-defence suggests that there is a whole piece of him and the world he has lived in that is missing. See if you can identify it. What might it say to him and to his friends, to us and ours?

4 A fresh voice

The entry of Elihu introduces a new dimension, so much so that many scholars have concluded that chapters 32—37 are by a different writer and an addition to the original text, but that is no reason to ignore his contribution.

First, Elihu is an outsider from a different world. He is young, has heard it all before, has a low esteem of his elders, has a clear picture of where he is and what he is, and is not backward at coming forward. Possibly he is a more intelligent member of the younger generation who sees the weakness of the inherited traditions and believes he (and his) have something better to offer. A less charitable view might see him as a new arrival from a sixth-form comprehensive perking up in the Oxford Debating Society. Either way, he is an outsider, with a distinctive style and language (more Aramaic).

Second, in terms of what he says, there is little that is fresh – a bit like a student's essay on God's justice, goodness and majesty (ticking all the familiar boxes) versus the self-righteousness of Job and his friends. But, as often, what he says is of less importance than his presence. Whereas the friends lecture Job, Elihu has a different approach. He goes out of his way to identify with Job (33:6) and calls him by his name. He also encounters Yahweh differently, referring to him as El (the shortened form of the divine name). By listening, he has heard what Job is saying, and while all the others have only confused things, Elihu has seen and heard Yahweh speaking and can see possible openings (albeit tiny ones) to new truth, suggesting that Yahweh may encounter us in more ways than one, such as dreams, visions and unexpected moments of insight.

Third, the immediate effect of Elihu's contribution is not obvious. Elihu's disappearance is as mysterious as his arrival, but there are at least two results. One, by focusing on what Job is missing, he has nudged open a new door. Two, when some of the sentiments of Elihu are echoed later in the divine speech, Job begins to hear and in the end finds satisfaction.

5 Seeing, not hearing

If Job has a question for God, God has a thousand for Job, mostly to remind him (and his friends) of their limited vision – the rest of the world outside their immediate preoccupation; so much they don't know, take for granted or don't think about, so sure are they of their own tiny world and (even more so) their limited understanding of how everything works. But, once again, the force of the divine speeches is not so much what Yahweh says. Little is gained by unpicking it verse by verse. The strength of Yahweh's response is in the way it presents an overall picture – clear, simple and unleashed on Job like a downpour in a thunderstorm – and the way in which he handles Job.

Confronted with a situation marked by the total absence of love, Yahweh puts all humanity in its place. The world is not just 'God and us', with the animals, the natural world and maybe the universe as an afterthought, in that order. Yahweh turns everything upside down to give us the universe, the natural world and (only then) humanity. Understanding the ways of 'God with us' begins with understanding ourselves and where we fit in the overall scheme of things.

What makes it work as it does for Job is Yahweh's method. Job's peers came bringing answers; Yahweh comes asking questions. His peers' tactics humiliated him, putting him down; Yahweh's tactics humbled him, accepting his sincerity, respecting his dignity, enabling him to find himself, while offering a different perspective that invites Job to think again and holds his feet to the fire until he does.

Readers searching the divine speeches for 'an answer' to Job's question are usually disappointed. There is none. Yahweh makes no attempt to solve Job's problem of suffering, and he excoriates the friends for misrepresentation (42:7), but for Job, once face to face with Yahweh, it no longer matters. Job does not want an explanation. He wants to be taken seriously ('a presence'). Once he gets that, Job can cope, as cold and rational *hearing* and *answers* give place to the warmth of *seeing* and *understanding*. A different Job. A different life.

6 Two worlds

Job's story demonstrates two ways of doing theology. One (Job's first speeches and the friends') moves from doctrine to the human condition; the other (Yahweh and Job's dialogue) moves from human experience to faith. The two worlds are totally different. Job's new life and family are not a reversion to his life before his encounter with God, and to see the restoration of Job's fortunes as unfair and unjust is to miss the point. In chapter 42 we come back to Job's family, but it is a very different family from the one we started with.

In chapter 1 Job is clearly a strong character both in the family and in the local community, but he is a detached father, and there is scant evidence that he relates closely to any of it. It is a dysfunctional family with no mood music, no atmosphere, no fun, no laughter, no spirit or emotion. Job has little regard for his wife, much less for her opinions. His children have no names and such human interaction as there is is confined to the eldest brother's house. Job is not part of it – he is on the fringe worrying about their spiritual well-being.

In chapter 42 we have revelry. His family has grown. He has brothers and sisters and lots of others who want to share his life. He even seems to have learned the art of hospitality (v. 11). You can give him a present, and he can receive it. Relationships matter. His daughters have names and are included in his inheritance. His family business is thriving. This is a totally different Job, and when Job changes we all change. Unreal? Maybe. Untrue?

At the beginning we suggested treating Job like a piece of music. A variation might be a play where, once you get to the end and grasp the whole, the rest falls away. Shakespeare's *A Winter's Tale* has a most unlikely ending, when a wronged Hermione, who has been dead for 16 years, comes to life. Unreal? Of course, and many critics have found it difficult, but transcending the literal is a gospel of hope. Hermione's restoration to life closes the circle, 'where what began with death and winter now ends with spring and a new birth' (from **sparknotes.com**). Much the same might be said of Job.

Guidelines

- Recall a moment when you have experienced Job's situation either as 'Job' or as 'friend'. How will reading Job help you to respond next time?

- If reading Job calls to mind a time when you faced a similar crisis, reflect on who helped, who didn't and with what result. If it calls to mind an occasion when you found yourself in the position of the friends, reflect on what you did and what you might have done better. This might make excellent material for roleplay if you belong to a study group.

- Reflect on the two worlds of Job (before and after). What other differences can you imagine? Now imagine the next ten years in the Job household.

- Imagine the conversation of the three friends on the way home. How might they have reacted to Elihu and what might they have learned?

- Would Job ever have appreciated 'the other world' had it not been for his sufferings? If the friends had known that, how differently might they have responded to him?

FURTHER READING

Robert Alter, *The Art of Biblical Poetry* (T&T Clark, 1990).

J. Gerald Janzen, *Job (Interpretation Bible Commentaries)* (Westminster John Knox Press, 1986).

Gordon Mursell, *Out of the Deep: Prayer as protest* (Darton, Longman & Todd, 1989).

1 Timothy

Ian Paul

The four letters of 1 and 2 Timothy, Titus and Philemon, gathered together at the end of Paul's writings in most Bibles, are often neglected, but they offer us some profound insights into Paul's thinking and practice. Alongside Paul's nine letters to seven churches, and if we include Hebrews as Pauline (which is probably mistaken but was a common assumption in the past), it means that we have 14 letters (2 x 7), and this appears to have been important in giving early readers a sense that they had a complete view of Paul's inspired writings.

1 and 2 Timothy, along with his letter to Titus, are usually labelled the 'pastoral epistles' because they are addressed to pastors who have oversight of some of the early Christian congregations in their area. There has been significant debate about whether they really were written by Paul, in part because of some distinct vocabulary which is different from Paul's earlier letters and in part because of what appears to be a different focus on questions of church order, reflected in Paul's concern for the appointment of 'elders'. But, as we shall see, there are many things in these letters which correlate not only with Paul's earlier concerns but also with those of Jesus and the other New Testament writers. Compared with the literature that we know from the second century, these letters look thoroughly Pauline, and much of their distinctive vocabulary is shared with the gospel of Luke and Acts, suggesting that Luke might have been involved in their writing. (Paul most often wrote his letters jointly with others. We also know that letters in the ancient world were usually dictated to a scribe; the scribe of Romans identifies himself in Romans 16:22.)

1 Timothy has an unusual structure, in that Paul happily moves from one subject to another, and from instructions to Timothy as a church leader to personal encouragements and instructions. He also returns to ideas more than once, so we will need to look out for connections. Although this letter contains ideas and texts that have become controversial and the subject of much debate, the whole letter is packed with insight and theological wisdom, and richly repays reading, study and application.

Unless otherwise stated, Bible quotations are taken from the TNIV or are my own translation.

1 The gifts of God

1 Timothy 1:1–11

Paul opens his letter without his customary extended thanksgiving, but with a summary of all that God has given him. In the encouragements and commands to come, Paul is not a self-appointed authority, but is a messenger sent with a royal proclamation (the heart of the meaning of 'apostle') by God himself, who, through Jesus' death and resurrection, is the one who saves us. This salvation is not yet fully realised; in Jesus we still have a future 'hope' that gives direction to our lives. But God has also given Paul, who was unusual (though not unique) in being single, a new family: Timothy is his 'genuine son' who will inherit Paul's legacy of teaching the gospel. Given the challenges he faces, Timothy will, alongside 'grace and peace', need God's 'mercy', these two letters being the only time Paul includes this term.

Disputes about doctrine began early – it is not a new problem! Paul is clear that speculative discussion that undermines faith needs a firm hand, but he is equally clear of the motive in doing so. This is not about control, power or the ego of the leader, but 'love' for others, exercised in a way that is transparent ('from a pure heart'), non-manipulative and without any hypocrisy ('sincere').

Paul does not see the grace of God in Christ as being opposed to the Old Testament law; rather, the gospel and the Spirit bring about the change that the law points to but cannot deliver. The summary here follows the shape of the ten commandments (Exodus 20), with the first four pairs of terms corresponding to the first five commandments and the remaining six terms corresponding to the last five, and links them with Paul's own cultural context. 'Kidnappers' (v. 10) refers to those who take people captive to be slaves, possibly through war – and so Paul condemns the central part of the Roman slave trade as forbidden by God. The term usually translated 'those practising homosexuality' is coined by Paul here and in 1 Corinthians 6:9, and translates the phrase from Leviticus 18:22, prohibiting same-sex relations regardless of form; refraining from sexual sin takes its place alongside all other forms of sin, neither emphasised nor ignored. The blessing of God in Jesus brings forgiveness, grace and transformation to every area of our lives.

2 God's mercy towards sinners

1 Timothy 1:12–17

I love hearing testimonies from people who have recently come to faith and hearing the change that God's grace has brought about. But I am also left with a nagging worry; after all, I was not a terrible sinner who had a dramatic change of direction! Does it matter that my story is so much less impressive?

Paul summarises for Timothy (and later readers like you and me) his testimony in this passage, and it contains two striking elements. On the one hand, Paul does not suffer from false modesty! He says his ministry is accomplished because of the 'strength' Jesus has given him, which elsewhere he describes as 'the mighty strength he exerted when he raised Christ from the dead' (Ephesians 1:19–20); he has been judged 'faithful', echoing Jesus' commendation of the 'good and faithful servant' (Matthew 25:21); and his ministry is by divine appointment. On the other hand, he is unswerving in describing his previous way of life 'as the worst of sinners'. In his violent zeal pursuing what he believed to be right, he was actually opposing what God was doing by his Spirit in this new Jewish movement that believed Jesus was the long-awaited Messiah. That meant he was not only taking the name of God in vain, but was actually persecuting Jesus himself in the form of his followers.

What could have bridged this enormous chasm in the two phases of Paul's life? The very thing that he emphasised to Timothy in his greeting: God's mercy. Paul deploys Old Testament language of sinning in 'ignorance', contrasted with wilful sin – but not to suggest that God's mercy was elicited by Paul's situation. Rather, his experience sits at the heart of the gospel: 'Christ Jesus came into the world to save sinners', a summary Jesus himself offers in Luke 19:10. The notion of a 'trustworthy saying' is not unknown in Greek literature, but Paul uses it in the pastorals to emphasise doctrinal and ethical statements of primary importance. We might not have lived a 'before and after' life to the same degree as Paul, but (he claims here) we are of the same kind. Each of us can receive the same forgiveness that Paul received; each of us has the same access to resurrection power for faithful living that he experienced.

3 The discipline of grace

Is our faith dependent on the work of God or our own effort? Is our effectiveness in ministry the result of God's power or our own focus and insight? Does our impact in shaping the world around us come about by God's sovereign work or our energetic engagement? Paul answers all these questions: 'Yes!'

The Holy Spirit does not appear to be as prominent in the pastorals as in Paul's other writing, but Paul is clear that Timothy's commissioning in ministry came through the Spirit's prophetic word through others, just as his own had done (Acts 13:2). But that commissioning then energises Timothy's own efforts, both in following Paul's 'command', a reference back to the need for sound doctrine in verse 3, and the general discipline of 'fighting the battle well'. This image is one Paul has used before (1 Corinthians 9:7; Philippians 2:25), one to which he will return later in the letter (1 Timothy 6:12; compare 2 Timothy 2:4), and the principle by which Paul has lived his own life (2 Timothy 4:7). Both Hymenaeus and Alexander are mentioned in 2 Timothy (2:17 and 4:14), though we know little about either. 'Handing over to Satan' might simply mean excluding them from the fellowship of God's people – but the goal is clear: that they will learn and hopefully be restored.

The tension between our role and God's sovereignty emerges again in Paul's instructions for prayer. In speaking about those in authority, Paul would echo Jesus' words to Pilate: 'You would have no power over me if it were not given to you from above' (John 19:11). We are therefore to pray for those in authority, that they would govern well, in accordance with God's will, and honour God's people. Yet we do this because it is God alone who is 'Saviour', in contrast to the claim made since Augustus that the emperor was saviour of his subjects. And Jesus did this not by oppression and power, but by standing in our place, giving his life as a ransom for us (Mark 10:45). In every age we are to live 'peaceful' lives, ones of determined loyalty to the only one who saves us.

4 Women and men learning and praying

For many Christians, these verses have become a battleground in the debate about women and men and their roles in ministry. We can clear the air by noting some important things about what Paul says and the way he says it.

First, there is a consistent symmetry in Paul's discussion about men and women. He wants men to 'lift holy hands' (in the common Jewish pose) in prayer, but the focus should not be on dispute and competition for prominence in the public space. 'Likewise' (*hosoutos*), women should not be competing to be the centre of attention when praying in public, with the elaborate hairstyles and adornment beloved of the elite wealthy in Roman society. (Paul cannot be talking in general terms here, as only the wealthy could afford the things he mentions.) The general reference to 'all men' means that Paul is talking to men and women in general, and not addressing issues between husbands and wives.

Second, Paul is encouraging women to 'learn', and so is taking one side in the more general first-century debate as to whether women should have access to education and understanding. The words for 'quiet' here do not mean silence (in Acts 11:18, Peter's audience are 'quiet' and praise God) but refer to the attentive listening required for learning – a widely praised virtue in Roman culture. The women are to submit to sound doctrine (not to men), just as the men should refrain from being argumentative.

Third, Paul does not use his usual language of 'command', as he has earlier, but is asking for a particular action to address a particular problem ('I am not permitting…'). The word translated '[usurp] authority' is not the usual word Paul uses (see 1 Corinthians 7:4); it is found only here in the New Testament and is very rare elsewhere. Prior to Paul, it means bully, oppress or even murder; after Paul, John Chrysostom uses it to describe men who wrongly 'domineer' their wives. Paul wants women to be confident in the truth, so they will not be 'deceived' like ill-taught Eve, but will know the salvation that came through *the* childbirth of obedient Mary – the mother of Jesus, who died 'to save sinners'. All this fits exactly with Paul's concern from the beginning for the teaching of sound doctrine, which will allow grace to do its work.

5 The life of a leader

Paul's instructions here have often been interpreted as the development of a hierarchy in the church, as focusing on the importance of certain offices, and as a later development away from Paul's earlier 'egalitarian' view of the church. Careful reading of the text shows that none of these things is true!

The role of the 'overseer' (*episkopos*, from which we derive our word 'bishop') doesn't appear to be any different from the 'elder' (*presbyteros*) mentioned later in 5:17, and the terms are used interchangeably. And there is no suggestion that the deacons (*diakonoi*) are subservient to the overseers. Seven outstanding leaders were chosen 'to serve' (*diakoneo*) in Acts 6:5, and one of these, Stephen, was a teacher and miracle-worker who became the first Christian martyr. Paul's letter to the Christians in Rome was carried there by Phoebe, the deacon (*diakonos*) of the church in Cenchreae near Corinth (Romans 16:1), and Paul addresses the 'overseers and deacons' in Philippi (Philippians 1:1).

It is striking that Paul offers no role description here. The language of 'overseer' suggests both having a broad view of things and making sure that the right things happen; the corresponding verb is translated 'See to it that...' in Hebrews 12:15. What matters in all of these leadership roles is not the office, nor any strategy, but the character of the leaders, whether they are men or women. (There is no grammatical reason to think that the 'women' in verse 11 are 'wives', and we know from Romans 16 that Paul recognised women as leaders.) They should be mature, so that their status does not go to their heads ('conceited... as the devil'), and they need to have a good standing in the wider world, so as not to bring the people of God into disrepute and harm the progress of the gospel ('the devil's trap') – most of the virtues here were ones praised in wider Roman culture. And their calling by God to these roles must be 'tested' by the community, just as Paul's was in Acts 13.

Everyone looks like a sheep from the front but like a shepherd from behind – we all have people we follow, but we also have people who follow us and look to us as 'leaders'. We all therefore need to be growing in maturity, learning how to teach others about the faith, and to keep in good standing with non-believers.

6 Personal leadership

The personal note in these verses is commonly seen as the turning point in Paul's letter to Timothy. Up until now, Paul has been making general points about the importance of doctrine, in response to false teaching, and emphasising the character and integrity of leaders. From now on, his comments are directed more personally to Timothy. Like other letter writers in the first century, Paul treats his letter as a substitute for his personal presence; letters would be read aloud and sent by a letter carrier who had been in the presence of the letter writer and could explain what was written.

Paul makes clear why he is so concerned about the integrity of the community of Jesus' followers: having been adopted into sonship (Romans 8:15), we are 'God's household' (so leaders need to be good household managers, 3:4); we are both citizens of the kingdom of God (the Greek meaning of *ekklesia*) and the new Israel of God (the meaning of *ekklesia* in the Greek Old Testament). We are not the 'foundation' of truth; there is only one foundation, comprised of Jesus himself (1 Corinthians 3:11), obedience to his teaching (Luke 6:49) and the apostolic message of both (Revelation 21:14). But God's people are both a 'pillar' and a 'mainstay' of this; if they are not living out the good news of Jesus, then others will not be persuaded. This integrity requires attention and effort, but in the end springs from what God has done in Jesus, and Paul's concise formula summarises what is universally agreed among true believers: the incarnation ('in the flesh'), the resurrection ('vindicated'), witness by the angelic presence at the tomb, the apostolic preaching reaching the whole known world and Jesus' ascension to the right hand of the Father.

But a prophetic word of the Spirit has warned that in 'later times' (which Paul, like Peter in Acts 2:17, seems to think have already begun) people will become obsessed by misleading rules about 'dos' and 'don'ts'. Just as in 1 Corinthians 7, Paul teaches that faith in Jesus redeems the material things of this age, while also anticipating the age to come. We rejoice in both marriage and singleness, in both sexual union and celibacy, in both feasting and in fasting.

Guidelines

- Paul seems to be at pains to hold together things that we are often in the habit of separating. Despite his own vision, energy and drive, he never sees himself as working alone, but he has nurtured strong and close relationships with others – in this case, his protégé Timothy. And there are constant reminders that Timothy needs to appoint and develop teams of leaders; for Paul, leadership is always plural. Timothy's call, equipping and ongoing ministry is in the context of the Spirit at work in the community of faith, and Paul makes repeated reference to this. So he encourages us to reflect: who are those who have nurtured us in faith? Whom do we nurture? Where are our communities of faith on which we depend and in which we hear from God?

- Paul also constantly holds together the sovereign work of God, and our energetic response of work and discipline. Whereas we might think that the more God is at work, the less we need to do, and vice versa, Paul sees the two running in parallel. The more confident we are in the work that God is doing, the more carefully we need to live a life of discipline and responsibility, ensuring that the work that God is doing within us and around us is not in vain. Where do we need to grow in confidence in what God is doing? And where do we need to look to ourselves as we receive God's work?

- Paul holds together God's teaching in the Old Testament scriptures and the new work God has done in the life, death and resurrection of Jesus. There is no doubt that Jesus offers a radical new revelation of who God is and what he is doing – a revelation which has turned Paul from sinner to saint and has changed the direction of his life. And yet Paul sees Jesus as the full revelation of the God he also sees revealed in the scriptures, and so the commandments of the Old Testament continue to offer a plumb line to measure the work of the Spirit in our lives. So how are we measuring up?

1 How to eat well, live well

1 Timothy 4:6–16

Paul continues to address Timothy personally, but he does so in the context of both general principles about the Christian life and what is needed in the community of faith. He gives directions about diet, exercise and healthy growth. In all these things, he contrasts the life of the faithful leader with those who deceived God's people with false teaching.

Having talked about literal food, Paul continues on the theme by talking about spiritual nourishment for Timothy and those who teaches. 'These things' include the affirmation about the goodness of this world as created by God, as well as the reality of spiritual conflict as the people and purposes of God face opposition. If Timothy teaches these twin truths, it will not only build up God's people, but will 'nourish' him as well; this is a meal shared by both student and teacher. Paul then changes the metaphor to that of the gymnasium, which is perhaps surprising given the negative view that Jews (and Christians) had of games, because the custom was that the competitors were naked (*gymnos*, hence the name of the training arena). And yet there is a lesson to be learned, as long as there is a spiritual struggle between the powers of this world and the will of God. The discipline of bodily training offers a pattern for godly living; while the gospel comes to us by the grace of God, and sound teaching comes from those who have been faithful before us, there is a decision needed on our part to remain disciplined as we hold to these truths.

The need to respond to God's grace with discipline is important enough to become another 'trustworthy saying', and it explains Paul's own approach to ministry. It leads Paul to urge Timothy in the strongest terms: 'Command… devote… be diligent… persevere'. This in no way negates the importance of the work God continues to do in Timothy; his gifting has come by the Spirit through a prophetic word and prayer, when the council of elders laid hands on him (compare Acts 19:6), not as any kind of ordination, but as an act of blessing and commissioning. And the people of God need to continually hear what God has to say, through the reading together of scripture when they meet, and through the ministry of Timothy and others in Spirit-led exhortation and teaching.

2 The practice of pastoral care

Paul switches from the more personal concerns of the previous section to practical issues in managing the Christian community. Although these commands seem much more ad hoc, they are built on consistent theological and pastoral principles. It appears that Timothy lacks confidence because of his relative youth (see 4:12, something also alluded to in 1 Corinthians 16:10), though the language used here would fit someone around the age of 40. It is clear from the contrast with 'younger men' that it is older men in general, rather than 'elders', who are in view. Timothy needs to be neither timid, lacking confidence, nor autocratic, letting the authority of God's call on him go to his head. Instead, he is to treat every group of people with respect and wisdom, being pure and being seen to be pure in all he does.

So far, Paul's instructions match the expectations of wider culture. But his instructions about widows have no similar parallel and appear to spring from Old Testament concerns about the vulnerable (since widows might have lost their financial and domestic security) and from practical issues in the light of the gospel, and Paul here blends two sets of concerns.

On the one hand, there are strong indications that responding to the gospel with faith in Jesus dissolves traditional family ties and creates a new kinship group. Thus Jesus claims priority of allegiance that had previously been given to family members ('let the dead bury their own dead', Matthew 8:22) and goes on to form a new family identity among those who respond to the good news ('here are my mother, my brothers, my sisters', Matthew 12:49). Paul echoes this in his reference to Timothy as his 'true son' (1 Timothy 1:2). Yet, while we still live in this age, though anticipating the life of the age to come, existing social structures, including family relations, cannot be ignored, and family responsibilities continue.

On the other hand, Paul seeks to hold together compassion and response to genuine need with the demand for responsibility which rejects the exploitation of generosity, just as he did in his much earlier letters ('those who don't work shall not eat', 2 Thessalonians 3:10). For both the giver and receiver of pastoral care, faith does not involve mere assent to doctrine, but is made evident in life and conduct.

3 Caring for those in real need

At first reading in a modern context, these instructions from Paul appear quite problematic. He appears to distinguish between the 'deserving' and the 'undeserving' poor among the widows; he sets the bar for being 'deserving' very high; and he seems to have a very negative view of the younger widows and their motivations. But we need to remember that Paul is not writing *to* us, even though his writings are included in scripture *for* us. Rather, he is writing to a specific person and a specific situation, and we need to understand that to make sense of this text.

Widows were viewed with some ambivalence in the Roman world. Although attitudes to women varied, in general respectable women were expected to marry and bear their husbands at least one child – not least because there were more men than women in society due to the abandonment of female babies and the mortality of women in childbirth. Unmarried women, of any kind, were depriving a Roman man of a wife! Older widows were a threat to the line of inheritance of a family, while younger widows were seen as potential temptresses and thus a threat to marriage. Yet widows were also financially vulnerable without the income of a husband to rely on.

Against that background, it is striking that Paul commands Timothy to make quite formal provision for this group – the language of 'make a list' would normally be used of soldiers enlisting in the army. The list of qualities of the 'deserving' widow doesn't include anything that Paul would not expect of all members of the early Christian community; they match quite closely the instructions at the end of his letters to churches. And he encourages those who can to marry again and raise a family, in line with normal expectations, and to take up significant responsibility – the language of 'managing their homes' is elsewhere used of men who are heads or masters of their households. All this is at a time when the churches are relatively small communities with few resources at their disposal.

It was said of church leader John Wimber that a member of his church came and complained that he had met a man in need of temporary accommodation and had tried to find a church official who could make some arrangement. 'No one would do anything,' the church member said, 'so in the end I had to take him into my own house. The church should do something about it!' Wimber replied, 'It sounds to me as though "the church" did!'

4 Biblical patterns for managing leadership

Paul returns again to questions of the organisation of community leadership; although he has just been discussing the pastoral questions relating to (older) women, the mention of 'leading' makes it clear that Paul is talking about those who have been appointed as elders – something that Paul has been concerned about since his so-called 'first missionary journey' (see Acts 14:23). The language of 'double honour' probably refers to financial provision, since the word Paul uses (*time*) refers to money in all its uses in Acts (for example, Acts 4:34; 7:16). Financial provision for those in gospel ministry featured from the beginning, Paul being a beneficiary of a gift while in Corinth and arguing for it in 1 Corinthians 9:7–14. Both there and here he justifies this by an appeal to 'scripture', in both places quoting from Deuteronomy 25:4. But here he adds a saying from the teaching of Jesus when he sent out the 70 on mission, and cites the version in Luke's gospel (Luke 10:7; compare Matthew 10:10), suggesting that Luke was already written and recognised as authoritative by the time of this letter.

Paul continues to draw on biblical principles, taken up by Jesus and others in the New Testament, in outlining the handling of elders. The requirement for two witnesses to offer reliable testimony comes from Deuteronomy 19:15 and was a test passed by the ministry of Jesus (John 5:32) but failed by his trial (Mark 14:59). And every issue around leadership needs to be handled without favouritism or partiality, treating each person by the same standard regardless of their appearance. This impartiality is a central quality of God that is to be imitated by those who worship him as disciples of Jesus. It is the basis of our love for neighbour, following the grace of God to all people (Matthew 5:45); it is reason that salvation in Jesus is for both Jew and Gentile (Acts 10:34; Romans 2:11); it undermines every human discrimination (Ephesians 6:9; James 2:9); and it is what gives us confidence when we face God's judgement (1 Peter 1:17). Paul's mention of 'God and Christ Jesus and the elect angels' (v. 21) is probably an allusion to the same theme of judgement, when both sins and good deeds, now hidden, will be made plain (compare Luke 12:3).

5 Transforming relationships

1 Timothy 6:1–10

It might look on first reading that Paul is uncritically affirming the practice of slavery – but a closer look shows that is not the case. He recognises the injustice involved, calling slavery a burdensome 'yoke' (compare the use of the term in Galatians 5:1; Acts 15:10). But the problem he is addressing is that, in a social setting where both masters and slaves are members of the Christian fellowship, their equal freedom in Christ appears to undermine the social order. Paul is concerned that this might look like a revolutionary threat that distracts from the gospel ('the teaching'), so he urges that the behaviour of slaves should be exemplary – at the same time as using of them the language that Jesus uses of all believers (Luke 22:25–27), so that they become an example of Christlike service to others, whether they are looking after others or are looked after by them (the language of verse 2 is ambiguous).

As Paul draws this letter to a conclusion, he returns to the previous contrast he made (in chapter 4, but going back all the way to 1:3) between those who cause division and controversy and those offering healthy teaching. In both of Paul's descriptions of good teaching, as 'healthy' and 'godly', their character reflects both the origin of the teaching and the effect they produce. They originate with Jesus, the one who is the source of our healing and health and the one who brings God's presence to us by his Spirit, and they therefore produce health and godly character. The issue here is not unity for unity's sake, not the control of the community by Paul or any other leaders, but faithfulness to the teaching of Jesus himself.

The slogans about money, contentment and human mortality have some parallels with sayings in Stoic philosophy, but these originate with Paul. Two are quoted in the second century by Polycarp, the martyred bishop of Smyrna, and they have found their way into English as proverbs – though Paul here says it is the *love* of money, not money itself, which is the root of all kinds of evil. The lesson here on finding contentment in all circumstances is something Paul teaches elsewhere (Philippians 4:12) and lived out himself; it is a wonderful antidote to our restless, consumer culture, where what we have is never enough.

6 The practice of reconciliation

1 Timothy 6:11–21

In Paul's closing summary, he reiterates many of the themes of this personal and pastoral letter. Paul writes to Timothy both as a leader responsible for the lives of others and as a disciple himself, for whom the new life in Christ must continue to be a living reality. Thus he is to 'command' others (v. 17), but he is also to ensure that he takes hold of eternal life for himself (v. 12), so that he is teaching to others only things that are true for himself. And while this faith is deeply personal, it is never individualistic; Timothy's 'good confession', his profession of faith, was made in the presence of the community of faith (v. 12), so there are others to support, encourage and pray for him, as well as to hold him to account.

As before, there is the constant tension between divine sovereignty and human responsibility. The eternal life is only Timothy's because of God's call on his life, and it is the gift of grace to him. God is the source of all life, as well as the source of all wealth and contentment (v. 17), and so he will be the judge of all when Jesus returns – an articulation of the consistent view of the New Testament's eschatology. Yet both Timothy and those he leads need to respond to God's call, his grace and his provision in holy living. This will not be easy, since we participate in a spiritual battle, and there is a sharp contrast between godly living and its alternative (v. 20). Thus Timothy must continue to exercise vigilance and self-discipline (v. 11).

And all this is rooted in the person of Jesus. It is Jesus who shares with God the oversight of our lives (v. 13); it is Jesus whose return will mark the coming of God to earth and the end of the age (v. 14); and it is Jesus who will share with God the final judgement and rule (note his title of 'King of kings and Lord of lords' in Revelation 19:16). Yet this Jesus understands our struggles, since he too was challenged by the powers that be in the person of Pilate, and kept faith. And his teaching continues to shape and equip us (compare v. 19 with Matthew 6:20).

Guidelines

If, in the first half of this letter, we saw Paul holding things together that we often separate, as we continue to read we also see him separate things that we can be in danger of confusing or keeping together.

The clearest distinction he makes is between healthy, godly teaching and false teaching that divides rather than builds up. Healthy teaching builds faith and nurtures the people of God – but it is also a blessing to those who teach it. It unites the people of God, draws them to Jesus and fills them with hope. By contrast, false teaching focuses on things that are ultimately of no importance; it causes people to take their eyes off Jesus and creates division among God's people. The challenge for Timothy is the challenge that faces us: how do we tell the difference? How can we discern the good from the bad – and be nurtured by the one while turning from the other?

Paul also sees a distinction between the people of God and the culture that they inhabit. The community of faith needs to be marked by a distinctive concern for those in need, a distinctive integrity among its leaders and a distinctive moral character rooted in the scriptures and the teaching of Jesus. But such distinctives do not imply social distance. Slaves and masters find their relationship transformed into a radical equality as fellow disciples, but this must not be interpreted as a threat to society. Leaders manifest the best qualities of their culture as well as the character created by the gospel.

Paul's hope is that women and men will learn and grow together, shaped by faithful teaching into the likeness of their faithful Saviour. Where do we need to grow in gospel distinctives, and where do we need to close the distance with our culture?

FURTHER READING

John Barclay, *Paul and the Subversive Power of Grace* (Grove Books, 2016).

Gordon Fee, *1 and 2 Timothy, Titus (New International Biblical Commentary)* (Hendrickson, 1984).

Ben Witherington, *Letters and Homilies for Hellenized Christians Vol 1: A socio-rhetorical commentary on Titus, 1—2 Timothy and 1—3 John* (IVP Academic, 2006).

Tom Wright, *Paul for Everyone: The pastoral letters* (SPCK, 2003).

Guidelines forthcoming issue

HELEN PAYNTER

We work with a long lead-time when we design the *Guidelines* notes, and in the forthcoming issue we will be offering you a combination of notes contracted by my predecessor David Spriggs and those that I have commissioned. Together, I think they combine to form a rich, deep and occasionally innovative selection of reflections which I hope you will find invigorating and soul-feeding.

We'll be tackling some of the knottier parts of the Old Testament. Pauline Hoggarth is leading us through the tricky book of Ezra. As always, I'm grateful for the careful, prayerful scholarship of those who are willing to grapple with the thorns. Alison Lo will give us a tour through 2 Kings – a personal favourite of mine. And I'm delighted that Carly Crouch is helping us to engage with the glorious scope and promises contained in the third section of Isaiah.

In the New Testament, Steve Motyer is continuing his much-appreciated tour of Mark, and, new to *Guidelines*, Rosalee Velloso Ewell has written very helpfully on Hebrews. And we have a rather wonderful set of notes on 1 Corinthians from Nigel Wright, which will take us through the Pentecost season.

And then there are two rather more innovative contributions. I don't want to say too much here, but just to whet your appetite that I think you'll be intrigued by a rather novel approach to Revelation, and a themed set of notes, written by Stephen Finamore and Phil Grasham respectively.

See you next time!

What the Bible means to me: Hazel Sherman

If the Bible didn't matter to me, I would have spent much of my ministry short-changing the congregations I have been called to serve! This might sound like a rather back-to-front way of responding to the question, but it is how I could describe the sort of relationship I have with this library of books and writings which we call the Bible. It matters as the church's classic text, in which all Christians share even as they argue about its interpretation.

Any trained teacher can impart information about a subject that neither excites them nor draws their commitment, but it will remain a discipline without relationship. For me, it is vital that my Bible reading has a relational aspect and that each time I open its pages or scroll down the screen, I expect that 'the Lord has yet more light and truth to break forth from his word' (George Rawson, 1807–89). However, there is no quality in the physical book that sets it apart from any other book. If I need to prop a chair up, a thick Bible will be just as useful as a large encyclopedia. I believe that the words of the Bible become the words of God *as I engage with them*. The 20th-century theologian Karl Barth once said something like this, and it strikes me as a vital insight. The Bible matters because it lives in the encounter with the reader or hearer yet is not constrained by that reader's response – not unlike God's own self.

The Bible matters because it invites me into worlds that are not my own and turns me back to my own context in gratitude for the life I live here. It invites me to quarry for the difference between the habits and dress of faith and the constant reaching-out of divine providence. It matters because it reveals God's age-old and extraordinary open adventure for the sake of the world and speaks to me of Jesus in whom God brings that adventure to fulfilment.

Why do I come to Jesus 'at the end' rather than at the beginning? Perhaps because that is one of the ways for me in which the Bible has come to matter most. When I thought I had to accept the Bible as God's only textbook before I could learn from it, my discipleship journey was mapped out in do's and do not's. But when I began to admit its awkward, difficult blend of history, poetry, laws and more, and when I began to realise that it was full of as many questions as answers, I began to discover Christ in a new way and the Bible as a vital component in the toolbox of discipleship. It accompanies me into the reading of any novel, film or art work which extrapolates themes of life and death, light and darkness, and all shades and circumstances in between. These aspects of our culture become even more fruitful when we hear the polyphonic echo of scripture in the background.

An extract from *Opening Our Lives*

Lent is not about giving up or taking up, but a radical opening up: the opening up of our lives to God's transformative kingdom.

That is the challenge Trystan Owain Hughes (author of *Living the Prayer*, BRF 2017) sets in *Opening Our Lives*. Through practical daily devotions he calls on us to open our eyes to God's presence, our ears to his call, our hearts to his love, our ways to his will, our actions to his compassion and our pain to his peace.

The following is an edited extract from a reading entitled 'Our call to recognise Jesus in ourselves', reflecting on Galatians 3:23–29.

Recently, I officiated at the funeral of a congregation member. Derek was such a lovely man. He was a quiet and modest character. I thought I knew him well, but it was only when I visited him at home a few months before his passing that I heard more about his life. It was then I realised the quiet, and quite beautiful, impact that Derek's faith had on him and subsequently on the world around him. He was working in sales in the Welsh steel industry when he won a scholarship with his company to undertake community work in Austria to build houses for refugees. He then returned to the UK to supervise the refurbishment of a school building for refugee children. After that, he felt he had a calling to work in the social work field, so he joined the Probation Service and remained there for the rest of his working life. Derek's impact on the young people on probation he helped went far beyond his own experience. In fact, I spoke to a number of people attending his funeral who, unbeknown to Derek himself, had completely turned their lives around due to his kind and caring influence.

Not all of us can leave such an evident impact on the lives of those around us. However, our faith should still be having a positive and loving effect on everyday situations, on the world around us and on the people with whom we come into contact. In our passage today, Paul reminds us of our radical call to live lives that reflect the life of Jesus. The uniqueness of first-century Christian baptism was that, as our passage states, converts were baptised 'into Christ'. The Jewish conversion ritual had no equivalent language. Paul is clear that, in baptism, we not only become one with each other, but also with Jesus.

A few years back, I attended a service in Llandaff Cathedral in Cardiff to celebrate 20 years of women priests in Wales. The preacher asked us to turn to the person next to us and trace the shape of the cross on their forehead. It was hugely moving, as it reminded us of our baptism and our calling to live as Christ did – bringing hope to our communities, peace to people's hearts and compassion to those who are suffering. We are, in baptism, marked with a cross, and, while people can't see the actual cross that was left on our foreheads with oil and water in our baptism, they should see that cross reflected in our daily lives.

In the Eastern Orthodox Church, it is stated that we become *christoi* through baptism – in other words, that we become 'Christs'. In one of the recent films in the Star Wars franchise, *Rogue One* (2016), a blind character, Chirrut Îmwe, relies on the Force to know when to shoot or to avoid bullets. He repeats a phrase continually: 'The Force is in me; I am in the Force.' As I sat and watched the film in the cinema, I was amazed to hear that phrase, because it is reminiscent of a meditation I have used for many years to remind me of my call to live out Jesus in my everyday actions – 'Christ is in me; I am in Christ.' That is, in a nutshell, what being called by Jesus is all about.

Yesterday we considered the challenge to see Jesus in other people. Today, though, we are reminded that, by how we act and by what we do, people will see Jesus in us. We will be, as today's passage puts it, 'clothed' with Christ. As such, while there is certainly a place for talking about faith and discussing doctrine, in reality we connect with people in a far more profound way by reflecting Jesus in our acts of compassion and our seemingly inconsequential words and deeds of kindness.

When I left my childhood home to go to university to study theology, my dad gave me his Bible – it was the Bible that had been given to him by his own father when he had left for theological college. Inside the Bible were scribbled these words: 'Don't become of so much heavenly value that you are of no earthly use.' Our call to live out the gospel each day is at the very heart of our faith. As Albert Schweitzer put it, on reflecting on his Christian ministry as a medic:

I wanted to be a doctor that I might be able to work without having to talk. For years I have been giving myself out in words… This new form of activity I could not represent to myself as being talking about the religion of love, but only as an actual putting it into practice.

A prayer to be prayed slowly and mindfully – allow each word and phrase to inspire your walk with God:

Lord Jesus,
You call us to become more like you,
Transform us into your likeness by helping us to recognise ways we can reflect your love,
While not all of us can do great things, in you all of us can do things with great love,
In your name,
Amen

To order a copy of this book, please use the order form on page 149 or visit **brfonline.org.uk**.

Develop a pattern of Bible reading, reflection & prayer

Come & See

Learning from the life of Peter

Stephen Cottrell

When we look at the life of Peter – fisherman, disciple, leader of the church – we find somebody who responded wholeheartedly to the call to 'come and see'. Come and meet Jesus, come and follow him, come and find your life being transformed. Like us, he takes a step of faith and then flounders, and needs the saving touch of God to continue becoming the person he was created to be. *Come and See* provides a pattern of Bible reading, reflection and prayer.

Come and See
Learning from the life of Peter
Stephen Cottrell
978 1 80039 019 5 £8.99
brfonline.org.uk

From Helen Paynter

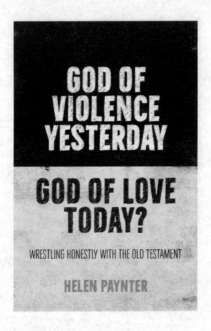

While acknowledging that there are no easy answers, in *God of Violence Yesterday, God of Love Today?*, Helen Paynter faces the tough questions head-on and offers a fresh, accessible approach to a significant issue. For all those seeking to engage with the Bible and gain confidence in the God it portrays, she provides tools for reading and interpreting biblical texts, and points to ways of dealing with the overall trajectories of violence.

God of Violence Yesterday, God of Love Today?
Wrestling honestly with the Old Testament
Helen Paynter
978 0 85746 639 6 £9.99
brfonline.org.uk

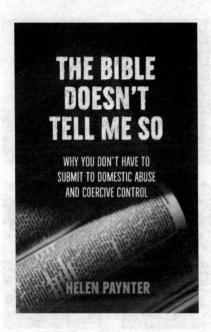

This book is addressed directly to women experiencing domestic abuse, and to those who seek to support them, including pastoral leaders, friends and support organisations. It debunks the myths – perpetuated by some abusers and, unwittingly, by many churches – which prevent women from getting out of harm's way. It helps them realise that the Bible does not belong to their abuser but is a text of liberation.

The Bible Doesn't Tell Me So
Why you don't have to submit to domestic abuse and coercive control
Helen Paynter
978 0 85746 989 2 £8.99
brfonline.org.uk

Holy Habits resources for church leaders

Holy Habits is an adventure in Christian discipleship based upon Luke's picture of the early church in Acts 2:42-47. It explores and encourages the practice of ten disciplines, or holy habits. These church handbooks are designed to help churches explore the habits creatively in a range of contexts and live them out in whole-life, intergenerational, missional discipleship.

Holy Habits church handbooks
Missional discipleship resources for churches
edited by Andrew Roberts, Neil Johnson and Tom Milton
£4.99 each
brfonline.org.uk

**Complete series
(for both sets of
resources):**

Biblical Teaching

Fellowship

Breaking Bread

Prayer

Sharing Resources

Serving

Eating Together

Gladness and
Generosity

Worship

Making More
Disciples

This Holy Habits Bible study group material has been created to help
churches explore the habits through prayerful engagement with the
Bible. Each book provides eight sessions of study material with a
Bible passage, reflection, group questions and community/outreach
ideas. There are also art and media links and prayers.

Holy Habits Group Studies
Leaders' guide
edited by Andrew Roberts
£6.99 each
brfonline.org.uk

BULK DISCOUNTS
available at
brfonline.org.uk

Mentoring Conversations

30 key topics to explore together

Tony Horsfall

A core resource for anyone involved in spiritual mentoring, this book provides a basis for spiritual conversation in a mentoring context through 30 short chapters structured around six key topic areas: Foundations; Steps to growth; Living out your faith; Going deeper; Staying strong; and Living with mystery. Each chapter begins with a Bible passage or text, followed by the author's comment on the topic, questions for discussion and scriptures for further reflection.

Mentoring Conversations
30 key topics to explore together
Tony Horsfall
978 0 85746 925 0 £9.99
brfonline.org.uk

To order

Online: **brfonline.org.uk**
Telephone: +44 (0)1865 319700
Mon–Fri 9.15–17.30

Delivery times within the UK are
normally 15 working days. Prices are
correct at the time of going to press
but may change without prior notice.

Title	Price	Qty	Total
Opening Our Lives	£8.99		
Come and See	£9.99		
God of Violence Yesterday, God of Love Today?	£9.99		
The Bible Doesn't Tell Me So	£8.99		
Mentoring Conversations	£9.99		

POSTAGE AND PACKING CHARGES			
Order value	UK	Europe	Rest of world
Under £7.00	£2.00	Available on request	Available on request
£7.00–£29.99	£3.00		
£30.00 and over	FREE		

Total value of books	
Postage and packing	
Total for this order	

Please complete in BLOCK CAPITALS

Title _____ First name/initials _____ Surname _____

Address _____

_____ Postcode _____

Acc. No. _____ Telephone _____

Email _____

Method of payment

❑ Cheque (made payable to BRF)   ❑ MasterCard / Visa

Card no. ⬚⬚⬚⬚ ⬚⬚⬚⬚ ⬚⬚⬚⬚ ⬚⬚⬚⬚ ⬚⬚⬚⬚

Expires end ⬚M⬚M ⬚Y⬚Y   Security code* ⬚⬚⬚   Last 3 digits on the reverse of the card

Signature* _____ Date _____ /_____ /_____

*ESSENTIAL IN ORDER TO PROCESS YOUR ORDER

Please return this form to:
BRF, 15 The Chambers, Vineyard, Abingdon OX14 3FE | **enquiries@brf.org.uk**
To read our terms and find out about cancelling your order, please visit **brfonline.org.uk/terms**.

The Bible Reading Fellowship (BRF) is a Registered Charity (233280)

BRF needs you!

If you're one of our regular *Guidelines* readers, you will know all about the impact that regular Bible study has on faith and ministry and the value of serious daily notes to guide, inform and challenge you.

Here are some recent comments from *Guidelines* readers:

'... very thoughtful and spiritually helpful. [These notes] are speaking to the church as it is today, and therefore to Christians like us who live in today's world.'

'You have assembled an amazingly diverse group of people and their contributions are most certainly thoughtful.'

If you have similarly positive things to say about *Guidelines*, would you be willing to share your experience with others? Perhaps you could give a short talk or write a brief article about why you find *Guidelines* helpful. You could form a *Guidelines* reading group, perhaps supplying members with their first copy of the notes. Or you could pass on your back copies or give someone a gift subscription. However you do it, the important thing is to find creative ways to put a copy of *Guidelines* into someone else's hands.

It doesn't need to be complicated and we can help with group and bulk buy discounts.

We can supply further information if you need it and would love to hear about it if you do find ways to get *Guidelines* into new readers' hands.

For more information:

- Email **enquiries@brf.org.uk**
- Telephone BRF on +44 (0)1865 319700 Mon–Fri 9.15–17.30
- Write to us at BRF, 15 The Chambers, Vineyard, Abingdon OX14 3FE

Enabling all ages to grow in faith

At BRF, we long for people of all ages to grow in faith and understanding of the Bible. That's what all our work as a charity is about.

- Our **Living Faith** ministry offers resources to help Christians go deeper in their understanding of scripture, in prayer and in their walk with God. Our conferences and events bring people together to share this journey, while our Holy Habits resources help whole congregations grow together as disciples of Jesus, living out and sharing their faith.

- We also want to make it easier for local churches to engage effectively in ministry and mission – by helping them bring new families into a growing relationship with God through **Messy Church** or by supporting churches as they nurture the spiritual life of older people through **Anna Chaplaincy**.

- Our **Parenting for Faith** team coaches parents and others to raise God-connected children and teens, and enables churches to fully support them.

Do you share our vision?

Though a significant proportion of BRF's funding is generated through our charitable activities, we are dependent on the generous support of individuals, churches and charitable trusts.

   If you share our vision, would you help us to enable even more people of all ages to grow in faith? Your prayers and financial support are vital for the work that we do. You could:

- Support BRF's ministry with a regular donation;
- Support us with a one-off gift;
- Consider leaving a gift to BRF in your will (see page 152);
- Encourage your church to support BRF as part of your church's giving to home mission – perhaps focusing on a specific ministry or programme;
- Most important of all, support BRF with your prayers.

Donate at **brf.org.uk/donate** or use the form on pages 153–54.

There is a time for everything...

There is a time for everything, and a season for every activity under the heavens: a time to be born and a time to die... a time to kill and a time to heal, a time to tear down and a time to build, a time to weep and a time to laugh...
ECCLESIASTES 3:1–4 (NIV, abridged)

I feel intimidated by the task before me: writing something now, in mid-June, that will still be of substance when you read it early next year. Yet, I have good cause for confidence.

While coronavirus has affected us all, some in ways that will never be forgotten, there is comfort to be found in the words of scripture. Ecclesiastes tells us that there is a time for everything – a season comes, and a season goes. Jesus warns us not to store up treasures for ourselves on earth, but rather to place our hope fully in the heavenly kingdom, where good things do not end and where every tear is wiped away.

These truths do not remove the pain we feel now. They do give hope beyond it.

Our work as a charity is to share timeless truths and an unswerving hope with a constantly changing world – work that requires we adapt to make a difference in every generation.

Much of what we do today – and God willing into the future – is funded by donations and gifts in wills.

I'd like to invite you to prayerfully consider whether you could support this work through a gift in your will. If you would like further information about leaving a gift in your will to BRF, please get in touch with us on **+44 (0)1235 462305**, via **giving@brf.org.uk** or visit **brf.org.uk/lastingdifference**.

Martin Gee
Fundraising manager

PS: Please be assured that whatever decision you reach about your will, you don't need to tell us and we won't ask. May God grant you wisdom as you reflect on these things.

Pray. Give. Get involved.
brf.org.uk

SHARING OUR VISION – MAKING A GIFT

I would like to make a gift to support BRF. Please use my gift for:

☐ Where it is most needed ☐ Anna Chaplaincy ☐ Living Faith

☐ Messy Church ☐ Parenting for Faith

Title	First name/initials	Surname

Address

	Postcode

Email

Telephone

Signature	Date

giftaid it You can add an extra 25p to every £1 you give.

Please treat as Gift Aid donations all qualifying gifts of money made

☐ today,   ☐ in the past four years,   ☐ and in the future.

I am a UK taxpayer and understand that if I pay less Income Tax and/or Capital Gains Tax in the current tax year than the amount of Gift Aid claimed on all my donations, it is my responsibility to pay any difference.

☐ My donation does not qualify for Gift Aid.

Please notify BRF if you want to cancel this Gift Aid declaration, change your name or home address, or no longer pay sufficient tax on your income and/or capital gains.

We will use your personal data to process this transaction. From time to time we may send information about the work of BRF that we think may be of interest to you. Our privacy policy is at **brf.org.uk/privacy**. Please contact us if you wish to discuss your mailing preferences.

Please complete other side of form ➔

SHARING OUR VISION – MAKING A GIFT

Regular giving

By Direct Debit: You can set up a Direct Debit quickly and easily
at **brf.org.uk/donate**

By Standing Order: Please contact our Fundraising Administrator
+44 (0)1865 319700 | **giving@brf.org.uk**

One-off donation

Please accept my gift of:

☐ £10 ☐ £50 ☐ £100   Other £ ☐

by (*delete as appropriate*):

☐ Cheque/Charity Voucher payable to 'BRF'

☐ MasterCard/Visa/Debit card/Charity card

Name on card

Card no. ☐☐☐☐☐ ☐☐☐☐☐ ☐☐☐☐☐ ☐☐☐☐☐

Expires end ☐M☐M ☐Y☐Y   Security code* ☐☐☐

*Last 3 digits on the reverse of the card
ESSENTIAL IN ORDER TO PROCESS
YOUR PAYMENT

Signature   Date

☐ I would like to leave a gift to BRF in my will.
Please send me further information.

Registered with

For help or advice regarding making a gift, please contact
our Fundraising Administrator +44 (0)1865 319700

FUNDRAISING **REGULATOR**

☚ Please complete other side of form

Please return this form to:
BRF, 15 The Chambers, Vineyard, Abingdon OX14 3FE

The Bible Reading Fellowship is a Registered Charity (233280)

GL0121

GUIDELINES SUBSCRIPTION RATES

Please note our new subscription rates, current until 30 April 2022:

Individual subscriptions
covering 3 issues for under 5 copies, payable in advance
(including postage & packing):

	UK	Europe	Rest of world
Guidelines 1-year subscription	£18.00	£25.95	£29.85
Guidelines 3-year subscription (9 issues)	£52.65	N/A	N/A

Group subscriptions
covering 3 issues for 5 copies or more, sent to one UK address (post free):

Guidelines 1-year subscription	£14.25 per set of 3 issues p.a.

Please note that the annual billing period for group subscriptions runs from 1 May to 30 April.

Overseas group subscription rates
Available on request. Please email **enquiries@brf.org.uk**.

Copies may also be obtained from Christian bookshops:

Guidelines	£4.75 per copy

All our Bible reading notes can be ordered
online by visiting **brfonline.org.uk/collections/
subscriptions**

GUIDELINES

Guidelines is also available as
an app for Android, iPhone and iPad
brfonline.org.uk/collections/apps

All our Bible reading notes can be ordered online by visiting
brfonline.org.uk/collections/subscriptions

☐ I would like to take out a subscription:

Title .... First name/initials .... Surname ....

Address ....

.... Postcode ....

Telephone .... Email ....

Please send *Guidelines* beginning with the May 2021 / September 2021 / January 2022 issue (*delete as appropriate*):

(please tick box)		UK		Europe		Rest of world
Guidelines 1-year subscription	☐	£18.00	☐	£25.95	☐	£29.85
Guidelines 3-year subscription	☐	£52.65		N/A		N/A

Total enclosed £ .... (cheques should be made payable to 'BRF')

Please charge my MasterCard / Visa ☐ Debit card ☐ with £ ....

Card no. ☐☐☐☐ ☐☐☐☐ ☐☐☐☐ ☐☐☐☐

Expires end ☐☐ ☐☐ Security code* ☐☐☐ Last 3 digits on the reverse of the card

Signature* .... Date ....../....../......
*ESSENTIAL IN ORDER TO PROCESS YOUR PAYMENT

To set up a Direct Debit, please also complete the Direct Debit instruction on page 159 and return it to BRF with this form.

Please return this form to:
BRF, 15 The Chambers, Vineyard, Abingdon OX14 3FE

To read our terms and find out about cancelling your order, please visit **brfonline.org.uk/terms**.

The Bible Reading Fellowship (BRF) is a Registered Charity (233280)

GL0121

GUIDELINES GIFT SUBSCRIPTION FORM

☐ I would like to give a gift subscription (please provide both names and addresses):

Title _____ First name/initials _____ Surname _____

Address _____

_____ Postcode _____

Telephone _____ Email _____

Gift subscription name _____

Gift subscription address _____

_____ Postcode _____

Gift message (20 words max. or include your own gift card):

_____

_____

Please send *Guidelines* beginning with the May 2021 / September 2021 / January 2022 issue (*delete as appropriate*):

(*please tick box*)	UK	Europe	Rest of world
Guidelines 1-year subscription	☐ £18.00	☐ £25.95	☐ £29.85
Guidelines 3-year subscription	☐ £52.65	N/A	N/A

Total enclosed £ _____ (cheques should be made payable to 'BRF')

Please charge my MasterCard / Visa ☐ Debit card ☐ with £ _____

Card no. ☐☐☐☐ ☐☐☐☐ ☐☐☐☐ ☐☐☐☐

Expires end ☐☐ ☐☐   Security code* ☐☐☐   Last 3 digits on the reverse of the card

Signature* _____ Date _____ /_____ /_____

*ESSENTIAL IN ORDER TO PROCESS YOUR PAYMENT

To set up a Direct Debit, please also complete the Direct Debit instruction on page 159 and return it to BRF with this form.

Please return this form to:
BRF, 15 The Chambers, Vineyard, Abingdon OX14 3FE

To read our terms and find out about cancelling your order, please visit **brfonline.org.uk/terms**.

The Bible Reading Fellowship (BRF) is a Registered Charity (233280)

You can pay for your annual subscription to our Bible reading notes using Direct Debit. You need only give your bank details once, and the payment is made automatically every year until you cancel it. If you would like to pay by Direct Debit, please use the form opposite, entering your BRF account number under 'Reference number'.

You are fully covered by the Direct Debit Guarantee:

The Direct Debit Guarantee

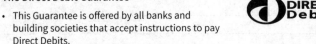

- This Guarantee is offered by all banks and building societies that accept instructions to pay Direct Debits.
- If there are any changes to the amount, date or frequency of your Direct Debit, The Bible Reading Fellowship will notify you 10 working days in advance of your account being debited or as otherwise agreed. If you request The Bible Reading Fellowship to collect a payment, confirmation of the amount and date will be given to you at the time of the request.
- If an error is made in the payment of your Direct Debit, by The Bible Reading Fellowship or your bank or building society, you are entitled to a full and immediate refund of the amount paid from your bank or building society.
- If you receive a refund you are not entitled to, you must pay it back when The Bible Reading Fellowship asks you to.
- You can cancel a Direct Debit at any time by simply contacting your bank or building society. Written confirmation may be required. Please also notify us.

The Bible Reading Fellowship

Instruction to your bank or building society to pay by Direct Debit

Please fill in the whole form using a ballpoint pen and return it to:
BRF, 15 The Chambers, Vineyard, Abingdon OX14 3FE

Service User Number: | 5 | 5 | 8 | 2 | 2 | 9 |

Name and full postal address of your bank or building society

To: The Manager	Bank/Building Society
Address	
	Postcode

Name(s) of account holder(s)

Branch sort code

Bank/Building Society account number

Reference number

Instruction to your Bank/Building Society
Please pay The Bible Reading Fellowship Direct Debits from the account detailed in this instruction, subject to the safeguards assured by the Direct Debit Guarantee. I understand that this instruction may remain with The Bible Reading Fellowship and, if so, details will be passed electronically to my bank/building society.

Signature(s)

Banks and Building Societies may not accept Direct Debit instructions for some types of account.

Enabling all ages to grow in faith

Anna Chaplaincy

Living Faith

Messy Church

Parenting for Faith

The Bible Reading Fellowship (BRF) is a Christian charity that resources individuals and churches. Our vision is to enable people of all ages to grow in faith and understanding of the Bible and to see more people equipped to exercise their gifts in leadership and ministry.

To find out more about our ministries and programmes, visit
brf.org.uk